One Dish

at a

Time

Valerie Bertinelli

One Dish at a Time

Delicious Recipes and Stories from My
Italian-American Childhood and Beyond

RODALE

Rodale books may be purchased for business or promotional use or for special sales. For information, please write to: Special Markets Department, Rodale, Inc., 733 Third Avenue, New York, NY 10017

Printed in the United States of America
Rodale Inc. makes every effort to use acid-free ♾, recycled paper ♲.

Recipe and food photographs © Quentin Bacon
Recipe food stylist: Mariana Velasquez
Recipe prop stylist: Lisa Lee
Lifestyle images on pages 8, 10, 40, 43, 54, 85, 86, 107, 132, 137, 143, 147, 176, 199, 205
Lifestyle photographs © Brian Bowen Smith
Lifestyle food stylist: Susan Sugarman
Lifestyle prop stylist: Dani Fisher
Val's hair: Roque
Val's make-up: Eric Bernard
Wardrobe stylist: Linda Medvene
Family candid photos courtesy of Val: pages v, x, xiii, 55, 109, 183, 229

Library of Congress Cataloging-in-Publication Data is on file with the publisher.

ISBN 978-1-60961-460-7

Distributed to the trade by Macmillan

2   4   6   8   10   9   7   5   3   1   hardcover

We inspire and enable people to improve their lives and the world around them.
rodalebooks.com

For my mom and dad,
with love and gratitude

ACKNOWLEDGMENTS

WRITING A COOKBOOK was always a dream for me, and this first one has been an exciting adventure. I was helped by a talented group of people, each of whom added a touch of expertise and a pinch of brilliance.

It started with my editor Kathleen Hackett, a woman of exceptional patience and knowledge. Without her, this book never would have been completed. Recipe developer, Lesley Porcelli, too, was instrumental. She nimbly translated "a dash of this and a knob of that" into precise recipes that taste just as they should: delicious. Photographer Brian Bowen Smith and his team shot amazing pictures at my California home and had way too much fun doing it. There, food stylist Susan Sugarman turned out sauces, sandwiches, and pastas just like my Nonnie, mother, and aunts did—with a lot of love. Prop stylist Dani Fisher set such lovely tables that I have repeated them since. In the studio, food photographer Quentin Bacon, food stylist Mariana Velasquez, and prop stylist Lisa Lee made a formidable team. They made every dish look like art.

Putting recipes and images—archival and new in this case—together is an art in and of itself and senior designer Kara Plikaitis did a beautiful job marrying the two. Executive director of art and design Amy King created a fantastic, vibrant cover. The executive team at Rodale clearly knows the recipe for taking care of authors and successfully publishing books. My best to Maria Rodale and the Rodale family. To Rodale Books publisher Stephen Perrine; Rodale Books and Healthy Living Group general manager Dave Zinczenko; associate publisher Beth Lamb; design director George Karabotsos; editorial director Elissa Altman; and publicity directors Yelena Gitlin Nesbit and Aly Mostel—a very big thank you. Senior managing editor Chris Krogermeier and senior project editor Marilyn Hauptly kept all of the moving parts on track as well as managing the copyediting and indexing of the book. Thanks to Angela Giannopoulos, assistant managing editor, and Rodale Test Kitchen's JoAnn Brader, manager, and Jennifer Kushnier, assistant manager, for crunching all of those nutrition numbers.

Special thanks to my pal Todd Gold. This is our third adventure in publishing, and I look forward to many more. The dear Clara Martinez helped me meet every deadline and more, and knows how to nudge me just enough to get me going. To Roque, Eric, and Linda who made me look *purdy* for the shoot; Jack and Marc, as always; Dan Strone at Trident Media Group; Lois, Rod, and all at GR&F; Jamie for all the hard work behind the scenes; everyone at Innovative; Heidi, Jill, Gabe and everyone at PMK for making it fun; and, of course, all the amazing women in my family and my dear, sweet girlfriends who have shared their passion for food and personal recipes over the years. They are the real secret ingredients here. Food is always best when shared with people you love.

CONTENTS

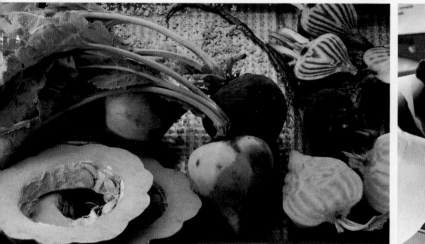

INTRODUCTION

I FELL IN LOVE with my husband, Tom, when we were making dinner. I had already met and liked him, but I'm talking about the moment when I felt the sweet flutter of desire and knew that one day soon I was going to say those three incredible words that as a single woman I uttered only to a bowl of pasta *alle vongole* or a slice of walnut banana bread: *I love you.*

We were at the home of my brother, Pat, and his wife, Stacy. We all were preparing the meal together. Tom and I had been assigned starters. He was making shrimp appetizers, and I was topping crostinis with mozzarella, prosciutto, and fresh basil leaves. As we worked, the two of us kept trading glances and helping each other. Walls came down as we touched and tasted each other's ingredients. Soon all I wanted to do was to kiss Tom, and it turned out he was thinking, "Wow, I could really spend the rest of my life with this woman."

Now I can't promise you that I know the recipe for finding love, but I do know that finding the right recipes frequently results in that special feeling you never want to forget. In *One Dish at a Time*, I have collected recipes from my life that fit that description. Each one represents a food memory, past and present. They have come from a lifetime of cooking, eating, and sharing meals with those I love. In many cases, the people have made the meal, but the meal has been what's made those occasions unforgettable—and that's what I am hoping to share with you and hoping you end up sharing with others.

You'll also find dishes that earned raves from Tom, his children, the ladies in my book club, and my son Wolfie. The influences here range from childhood memories to recent travels. I have included recipes from family and friends, like my girlfriend Lynn's brownies. One bite of those and you'll feel like you've known her for years, too.

In my mind, a good cookbook is about relationships. It's a collection of love stories. These are my love stories, beginning with my memories of being in my Aunt Adeline's basement kitchen as she, my grandmother, my Aunt Norma, and my mother made dinner for the extended family. They worked on a large table, kneading and rolling dough for gnocchi and cappelletti. Sauce simmered on the stove, and the air was infused with garlic. You want to know what love smells like? It smells like that basement.

My father recently sent me my Nonnie's rolling pin. It's one of my most treasured possessions, as are my mother's recipes. She wrote them down for me, but the truth is, most times she didn't look at recipes. When I was growing up, she cooked three meals a day. The kitchen was her office, the heartbeat of our home, and no matter how many people were at the table—our family of five or more if we had friends over—she knew what to do. Mrs. Van Halen was like that, too. When Ed would go on tour after we were first married, I would spend the night at his parents' house, and in the morning his mother made the most amazing coffee I had ever had, which holds true to this day. She put everything in a French press—coffee, milk, sugar, and secret ingredients. I've spent years trying to duplicate it and crying over my inability to re-create that magical taste. Wolfie still kids me about it.

Unfortunately, you won't find her coffee in this book. She never wrote down the recipe, and I'm someone who still needs to follow a recipe. I aspire to the level of culinary skill where I can open the fridge and, *sans* recipe, whip up the kind of meals that I'm sharing with you here. My girlfriend Suzanne can do that and I marvel at it. She's the one who reawakened the foodie in me and put me on the road to respecting and appreciating food again. Slowly but surely I'm getting there.

As you know, I've been public about my weight issues and eating problems, which many of us share. As a child, I loved food. It conveyed feelings of family, comfort, and safety. Later, as an adult, I chased those same feelings and used food as fuel to feed my emotions, to block bad feelings, and sometimes to punish myself. In the morning, I'd swear to be faithful to my broccoli and fish all day, and then cheat on them at night with pepperoni pizza. The guilt! The unhappiness! The unwanted pounds! I lost precious time to counting calories instead of appreciating the exquisite simplicity of using food to nourish my body and feed my friendships.

One Dish at a Time is not a diet book. Instead, it assumes we all have learned, or are in the process of learning, moderation rather than deprivation. This book is about appreciating, celebrating, and enjoying good food, not being afraid to eat it. It reflects my improved and healthy relationship with mealtimes. Where I once used food to hide the worst of me, I now use it to share the best of me. My hope is that you find as much pleasure in making the dishes that follow as I took in creating them.

Mangia bene!

PS—Let someone else do the dishes.

Italian Sponge Cake

12 eggs - seperated   1 lb. xxxx sugar
2 cups cake flour   4 tsp. baking powder
1 tsp. salt   2 tsp. vanilla

Beat egg whites till stiff - set aside. Add sugar
to yolks till creamy. Add sugar
and beat together. Fold
alternating with
Pour ba

late pudd

th 3 tbsp

9/1/

Dec. 24, 57

Recipes
Nancy Bertinelli

A STONE PRODUCT®

90

A PRODUCT OF Westab DAYTON 2, OHIO

ingredients, mixing well. Chill, Shape
dough into 1" balls, roll in wheaties. Place each
2" apart on ungreased cookie sheet and
p with candied cherry.

Breakfast

Morning is about
indulgence, not denial.

I WAKE UP LOOKING forward to breakfast. Big surprise, right? Lately, I will cook up an egg and place it on top of a slice of high-quality, protein-infused bread, and that's my breakfast, along with coffee and my crossword puzzle. It's easy, it's healthy, it makes me feel good, and it leaves me satisfied. But generally I'm not a one-kind-of-breakfast gal. Sure, I get into routines, especially when I work, but I like variety. I like ease and practicality, too. (That's more of a life philosophy than a requirement for breakfast.) My schedule will vary from having to get up at 5 a.m. for a 6 o'clock call time on the set to being able to sleep in, and my breakfasts will reflect my schedule or lack of one, particularly on the weekends, when I have the time to linger at the table and luxuriate in my food choices.

As you will discover, the breakfast recipes I have included here range from different kinds of pancakes to various uses for eggs to muffins and a super-healthy smoothie. I am leaving simple things like toast and a bowl of fruit to you, though I've had mornings when I could have used the most basic instructions: *Hold the knife in your right hand. Use your left hand to hold the butter dish so it doesn't run away* . . .

By the way, I'm a fan of real butter. I will not use margarine. My mother has given me recipes from 30 years ago that call for margarine, but I don't make those. Using butter is a little thing, there is a tad more fat, but it makes a significant difference in taste and quality. I would rather spend 15 more minutes on the treadmill and enjoy butter's rich texture and flavor than deny myself.

To me, morning is about indulgence, not denial. I have heard that it's the best time of day to have sweets. Unfortunately for me, I like them late at night, and I often have to slap myself silly to keep from eating them. Everyone is different, though. You have to listen to your body, especially in the morning when the day is new and full of possibilities. Do you feel like grains? Do you feel like the tangy freshness of fruit? Do you need the hug that you only get from eggs Benedict?

I wake up assuming that I am going to be healthy with my meals all day, and I want to nourish that feeling, not derail it. Why do otherwise? Laziness? That's not an excuse. This is *your* time. If brunch is the bubble bath of meals, a Monday through Friday breakfast is a refreshingly hot shower. I feel best when I start my day off with a protein and carb combo. I wake up with the desire to be physical, and as a result I crave fuel. It's probably because I've put working out in my daily routine in the last few years and my metabolism has changed for the better.

I also crave the hugs my grown-up son still gives me when I make him his favorite breakfast, Pumpkin Pancakes (page 9), as I have done since he was a little boy, and that's why I included the recipe. Nothing wrong with some affection for mama at the breakfast table. It beats sweetener in my coffee. I also love taking leftovers out of the fridge. I must admit I feel so clever everytime Tom and I transform asparagus and broccoli from the night before into an egg white frittata. I know it's not rocket science. It's not even culinary science. It's breakfast. But it's delicious. And that's the point.

Challah French Toast

To this day, I can't make this without thinking back to Wolfie's elementary school days, when I made it almost every weekend—the sweet solution for using up whatever slightly stale sandwich bread happened to be left after the week's lunches. Now I like to use challah or Hawaiian sweet bread (also known as Portuguese sweet bread on the East Coast). If you want to slenderize this classic brunch dish, just use egg whites, 2% milk, and a few extra drops of vanilla. Rather than pour maple syrup—always the real stuff—all over them, put the syrup in a small finger bowl and cut the toast into thin rectangles for dipping. Wolfie always loved it that way.

WHISK TOGETHER THE eggs, milk, vanilla, nutmeg, cinnamon, and salt in a medium bowl. Spread the bread slices in a large glass baking dish (they may overlap) and pour the egg mixture over them. Let sit for about 2 minutes, then flip the bread slices over and let sit for 2 minutes more.

Preheat a large well-seasoned cast-iron or nonstick skillet over medium heat. Add enough butter just to coat the surface of the pan. Working in batches, slide the bread slices into the pan and cook until golden brown, $1\frac{1}{2}$ to 2 minutes per side. Transfer to a warmed platter. Tap confectioners' sugar through a sieve onto the French toast and serve warm with the maple syrup.

Per serving (when serving 4): *427 calories, 13 g protein, 72 g carbohydrates, 9 g total fat, 3 g saturated fat, 1 g fiber, 532 mg sodium*

Per serving (when serving 6): *391 calories, 13 g protein, 63 g carbohydrates, 19 g total fat, 3 g saturated fat, 1 g fiber, 531 mg sodium*

YIELD

Serves 4–6 (makes about 12 ½-inch slices)

5 large eggs

1 cup whole milk

1 teaspoon vanilla extract

¼ teaspoon nutmeg

¼ teaspoon ground cinnamon

¼ teaspoon kosher salt

1 pound challah loaf, sliced into ½"-thick slices (save the ends for another use)

1 teaspoon unsalted butter for the skillet

Confectioners' sugar

Warm maple syrup

LEMON CURD PANCAKES

YIELD

Makes about 30 silver-dollar-size
pancakes and 1 cup lemon curd
Serves 6

LEMON CURD

4 large egg yolks

Grated zest of 1 lemon

1/3 cup freshly squeezed lemon juice
(from about 1 1/2 lemons)

1/2 cup sugar

Pinch kosher salt

5 tablespoons unsalted butter,
chilled

PANCAKES

1 cup all-purpose flour

2 tablespoons sugar

1 teaspoon baking powder

3/4 cup whole milk

1 large egg, lightly beaten

Zest of 3 lemons, grated, plus more
for garnish

1/2 cup (4 ounces) ricotta cheese

Unsalted butter for the skillet

Crème fraîche (optional)

Give me any breakfast dish that makes liberal use of lemons. These are a special treat, one that I make for Sunday brunch when the lemons on my trees are at their peak. The original recipe, from an inn in Sonoma, called for cottage cheese, but being Italian, I couldn't help but switch it out for ricotta. Making lemon curd is easy, but you can also buy good-quality versions at specialty markets.

TO MAKE THE LEMON CURD: Combine the egg yolks, lemon zest and juice, sugar, and salt in a medium saucepan. Whisk to thoroughly incorporate. Cook over medium heat, whisking nearly constantly, until the mixture thickens enough to coat the back of a spoon, about 20 minutes.

Take the saucepan off the heat and whisk in the cold butter, 1 tablespoon at a time, until melted and incorporated. Transfer the curd to a bowl and press plastic wrap directly against its surface to prevent a skin from forming. Refrigerate until firm, at least 1 hour.

TO MAKE THE PANCAKES: Meanwhile, whisk together the flour, sugar, and baking powder in a large bowl. Whisk in the milk, egg, and zest until incorporated. Using a rubber spatula, gently fold in the ricotta.

Preheat a large well-seasoned cast-iron or nonstick skillet over medium-high heat, and add enough butter to just coat. When a drop of water thrown into the skillet bounces across the surface vigorously, add heaping tablespoon-size dollops of batter, allowing enough room between each for them to spread slightly. Cook until the bubbles begin to pop and hollow out on the surface of the pancakes, adjusting the heat as necessary, about 2 minutes. Flip and cook for about 1 minute more. Serve garnish with the zest, curd, and crème fraîche (if using).

Per serving: *349 calories, 8 g protein, 40 g carbohydrates, 18 g total fat, 10 g saturated fat, 1 g fiber, 150 mg sodium*

A Good, Long Run

I WAS GETTING SET to run my first half-
marathon when I ate Lemon Curd Pancakes
(page 7) for the first time. At the time, I was
setting goals for myself, and this half-marathon
was one of them. I had only started running the
year before. My trainer said he was going to teach
me how to run. I said, "Oh right." But he did, and
we worked our way up from a 10-minute run to a
full marathon. On the night before the race, I did
what all marathon runners do and carb loaded.
I had been on a strict diet, but I wanted to eat
something decadent before the race. I saw the
pancakes on the menu at the Sonoma Fairmont
Mission Inn where I was staying and immediately
said, "I can have these. I'm running 13 miles
tomorrow." I beat Tom by 8 minutes! Not only
were the pancakes amazing, but my time was, too.

PUMPKIN PANCAKES

Wolfie *looooves* pumpkin pie the way I love lemons. Of course, I always make it (see page 207) for Thanksgiving, which means I tend to overbuy the canned pumpkin. I'll take the aroma of cinnamon, ginger, and cloves wafting through the house anytime, especially around the holidays, which is when I'm most likely to make these moist, fragrant pancakes. Folding in the whipped egg whites gives them a wonderful lightness.

YIELD

Makes about 16 / Serves 4 for brunch or 8 for breakfast

1 cup all-purpose flour

2 tablespoons sugar

1 teaspoon baking powder

$\frac{1}{2}$ teaspoon ground cinnamon

$\frac{1}{2}$ teaspoon ground ginger

Pinch ground cloves

$\frac{3}{4}$ cup whole milk

2 large eggs, separated

$\frac{1}{2}$ cup puree solid-pack pumpkin

$\frac{1}{4}$ cup vegetable oil

Unsalted butter for the skillet

Warm maple syrup

COMBINE THE FLOUR, sugar, baking powder, cinnamon, ginger, and cloves in a bowl and whisk to combine. Whisk in the milk, egg yolks, pumpkin, and oil until just combined. In the bowl of a standing mixer fitted with the whisk attachment, beat the egg whites on high until they hold stiff peaks, about 2 minutes. Using a rubber spatula, gently but thoroughly fold the whites into the batter.

Preheat a large well-seasoned cast-iron or nonstick skillet over medium-high heat, and add just enough butter to coat. When a drop of water thrown into the skillet bounces across the surface vigorously, add $\frac{1}{4}$-cup dollops of batter, allowing enough room between each for them to spread slightly. Cook until the edges appear cooked, adjusting the heat as necessary, about 3 minutes. Flip and cook about 2 minutes more. Serve warm with the maple syrup.

Per serving (when serving 4): *467 calories, 8 g protein, 63 g carbohydrates, 21 g total fat, 5 g saturated fat, 2 g fiber, 170 mg sodium*

Per serving (when serving 8): *285 calories, 4 g protein, 45 g carbohydrates, 11 g total fat, 3 g saturated fat, 1 g fiber, 87 mg sodium*

Egg White Breakfast Burrito

A film set is a tough place to be on a diet—there are always yummy smells coming from the catering truck first thing in the morning, and that pretty much sets the tone for the day. I'm sure I had my first breakfast burrito back in the '80s during one of my shoots, and I'm certain it wasn't healthy—scrambled eggs (yolk and white), thick slabs of crispy bacon, American cheese, and full-fat tortillas. These days, I've learned to take the calories down without sacrificing the flavors that bring me back to that time. This is still my go-to food on work mornings—it's the best portable breakfast there is. I can't live without Dominic's Salsa (page 32) on it. When you have a big batch of this salsa on hand, the burrito is a breeze to whip together, although it's also great with Tabasco Chipotle Pepper Sauce or Crystal Hot Sauce. This recipe makes one serving, but it can be multiplied to make as many as you need.

1 low-fat whole wheat tortilla (8" diameter)

1 slice lower sodium center-cut bacon

2 egg whites, whisked together

Hot sauce

¼ cup grated extra-sharp Cheddar cheese

2 tablespoons Dominic's Salsa (page 32)

Freshly ground black pepper

PREHEAT THE OVEN to 200°F and place the tortilla on the oven rack to warm.

Meanwhile, heat a nonstick skillet and lay the bacon in the pan. Cook until it's done the way you like it—I like mine crispy—then remove and set on a paper towel. Drain most of the bacon grease, leaving a tablespoon or so in the pan.

Add the egg whites to the skillet. As they begin to solidify, move the eggs around the pan with a rubber spatula so that the liquid parts are exposed to the heat. Add hot sauce to taste. Remove the skillet from the heat just before the eggs are fully cooked.

Place the warm tortilla on a plate and sprinkle with the cheese. Lay the bacon on top of the cheese. Arrange the eggs down the middle on the bacon. Top with the salsa, season with the salt and pepper, and roll into a burrito. Serve with hot sauce and enjoy while learning your lines for the day!

Per serving: *283 calories, 23 g protein, 13 g carbohydrates, 18 g total fat, 10 g saturated fat, 8 g fiber, 550 mg sodium*

Eggs Benedict Rx

YIELD

Serves 1

2 thin slices deli ham

2 tablespoons distilled white vinegar

2 large eggs

¼ cup dry white wine

2 tablespoons freshly squeezed lemon juice

3 tablespoons unsalted butter, cut into small pieces

Kosher salt and freshly ground black pepper

2 whole wheat 100-calorie English muffin halves, toasted

1 tablespoon chopped fresh chives

Hollandaise is ridiculously fattening, I know. Every now and then, I'll order it off a menu, but at home, when the craving hits, I'll make my version for Tom and me. The sauce is a simple emulsion of butter with white wine and lemon juice—no egg yolks. The thing is, you don't need a lot of any sauce if you cook the eggs perfectly, meaning nice and runny. That way, the yolks moisten the crispy English muffins perfectly. This recipe makes 1 serving with two English muffin halves, but, like a martini, one is really enough!

COOK THE HAM in a small skillet over medium heat until browned on both sides. Set aside.

Fill a medium saucepan with a tight-fitting lid with 2" of water. Add the vinegar and bring to a boil. Meanwhile, crack each egg into separate small heatproof mugs. Bring the boiling vinegar water to a simmer and gently lower the mugs all the way into the water. Carefully remove the mugs and leave the eggs behind. Cover and simmer the eggs 3 minutes. If the yolks appear underdone for your liking, continue cooking them for 1 minute more. Remove them with a slotted spoon to a paper towel-lined plate.

While the eggs simmer, combine the wine and lemon juice in a sauté pan and bring to a boil over high heat. Let boil 1½ minutes. Reduce the heat to low, then whisk in the butter, piece by piece, allowing each to emulsify before adding the next. Turn off the heat and season with salt and pepper.

Top each English muffin half with a piece of ham, followed by an egg. Drizzle with the sauce and sprinkle chives over the top. Serve warm.

Per serving: *622 calories, 20 g protein, 33 g carbohydrates, 45 g total fat, 25 g saturated fat, 9 g fiber, 682 mg sodium*

No-Crust Quichettes

I started making these years ago when I decided to go on a low-carb diet. Even though I now don't believe in removing any one thing from my diet, these are still a part of my repertoire because they are just so good. Mini quiches are yet another good way to use what happens to be in the fridge's crisper bin. I generally serve two per person, but more generous appetites might call for more. Serve these atop a lightly dressed plate of greens.

PREHEAT THE OVEN to 350°F. Lightly coat 12 cups of a muffin tin with olive oil.

In a large bowl, combine the broccoli, bacon, cheese, eggs, cream, paprika, salt, and pepper. Stir until thoroughly incorporated. Divide the mixture evenly among the 12 muffin cups. Bake until just set, about 25 minutes. Cool on a rack. Use a butter knife or small offset spatula to nudge the quichettes from the pan. Serve warm.

Per quichette: *261 calories, 18 g protein, 4 g carbohydrates, 19 g total fat, 9 g saturated fat, 1 g fiber, 630 mg sodium*

YIELD

Makes 12 (2½") quichettes

Olive oil for the muffin tin

2 cups cooked broccoli florets, chopped into ½" pieces

6 slices bacon, cooked and crumbled into small pieces

½ cup grated hard cheese, such as Manchego, Cheddar, Pecorino Romano, or Parmigiano-Reggiano

6 large eggs, lightly beaten

½ cup light cream

¼ teaspoon hot paprika

¼ teaspoon kosher salt

Freshly ground black pepper

LEFTOVER VEGGIE FRITTATA

YIELD

Serves 2–4

1 tablespoon extra-virgin olive oil

1 cup cooked mixed veggies, such as asparagus, spinach, cherry tomatoes, Swiss chard, mushrooms, broccoli, or cauliflower

4 large eggs, beaten with kosher salt and freshly ground black pepper

2 ounces goat cheese, crumbled

2 tablespoons chopped fresh herbs, such as chives, basil, parsley, tarragon, chervil, dill, or mint

This is the perfect clean-out-the-refrigerator dish, although everyone you serve it to will be none the wiser. Combine it with a salad of fresh greens and toast (and a strip or two of bacon, if you want to indulge) and—voilà—brunch is ready. I typically set the frittata on the table and serve it right out of the skillet, but you can just as easily slide it onto a cutting board and present it at the table, ready to cut into wedges. If you want to lighten it up a bit, use two whole eggs and just the whites of three others.

PREHEAT THE BROILER.

Warm the oil in a small well-seasoned cast-iron or nonstick ovenproof skillet over medium heat. Add the vegetables and sauté until warmed through. Add the eggs, stir, and let cook until firm around the edges. With a spatula, lift the edges and tilt the pan to allow the uncooked portion of the eggs to run into the bare pan beneath the spatula. Add the goat cheese and herbs, stir slightly to incorporate, and continue to cook until the edges of the frittata are firm (the center will still be jiggly).

Transfer the pan to the broiler and cook until golden brown on top, about 2 minutes. Allow to sit for 2 minutes, then run a knife or a thin spatula around the edge of the frittata. Cut in wedges and serve straight out of the skillet, or slide it out of the pan onto a cutting board, cut in wedges, and serve.

Per serving (when serving 2): *298 calories, 19 g protein, 6 g carbohydrates, 22 g total fat, 8 g saturated fat, 2 g fiber, 332 mg sodium*

Per serving (when serving 4): *149 calories, 10 g protein, 3 g carbohydrates, 11 g total fat, 4 g saturated fat, 1 g fiber, 166 mg sodium*

BAKED SCOTCH EGGS

YIELD

Serves 6

6 large eggs, in the shell

1 pound bulk hot Italian sausage

2 large eggs, beaten

Kosher salt and freshly ground
    black pepper

1 cup panko bread crumbs

In my book, Scotch eggs are the ultimate "food as love" kind of dish, which is why I first made these when Tom moved in with Wolfie and me. A special breakfast seemed just the right way for all of us to bond. It was my way of encouraging lots of talking and lingering. Serve these with apricot or mango chutney or orange or lemon marmalade.

FILL A LARGE saucepan with a tight-fitting lid with 2" of water. Place the 6 eggs in the saucepan and bring to a boil over medium-high heat. Immediately turn off the heat and cover the pan with the lid. Let sit for 9 minutes. Transfer the eggs to a colander and rinse under cool water. Gently peel.

Preheat the oven to 400°F.

Divide the sausage into 6 mounds. Enclose each egg in a mound of sausage, smoothing it in place to enclose the egg completely. Set on a baking sheet and refrigerate for 10 minutes.

Season the beaten eggs with salt and pepper. Put the panko in a small bowl. Roll each sausage-covered egg in the beaten egg, then roll in the panko until completely covered. Return to the baking sheet and refrigerate for 10 minutes more.

Bake the eggs until the sausage is cooked through and the panko is golden, about 40 minutes. To eat, slice the egg in half, lengthwise.

Per serving: *394 calories, 21 g protein, 8 g carbohydrates, 31 g total fat, 11 g saturated fat, 0 g fiber, 754 mg sodium*

MY KITCHEN

ONE OF MY FAVORITE restaurants has a bar designed to let you look into its open kitchen. Tom and I will often stop there for a glass of wine and an appetizer just so we can watch the chefs in action. Studying their skilled movements is pure entertainment. I also enjoy simply peering into their kitchen, a workshop that's practical and magical. I often wonder what great chefs have in their home kitchens. For that matter, I am curious about people's kitchens in general. I once heard Julia Roberts wax lovingly about her kitchen. Does she have a bowl of fruit on the counter? Chips in the cabinet?

Maybe I'm a tad nosey, but I think you learn something about people from what they have on their counters and in their fridge and pantry. As for my kitchen, it's in the center of the house, between the living room and my library, and adjacent to the stairs leading to our bedroom. I have a large center island where I lay out the newspaper in the morning, sip my coffee, eat breakfast, and start the crossword puzzle. I usually have separate bowls on the counter, one for fresh fruit, another for vegetables, and a third for tomatoes, onions, and garlic.

I have the triangle that experts suggest: the sink, refrigerator, and stove positioned so that I take the fewest steps possible among them. For years I had wall ovens, but now my oven is beneath the stove and I like it better. I'm a little touchy about my fridge. People make fun of me for having an inordinate number of condiments. But it's true. I generally have three or four different kinds of hot sauces; a similar number of olives and pickles, both sweet and hot; and various dressings. Capers are always in there, too.

It wasn't always like this. My first kitchen, back when I was 19, had a few utensils, a pot, and some pans, and my staples were pasta, powdered soup, broccoli (over which I melted Cheddar cheese), and Cheetos. I think about those days every once in a while. Mostly I wonder why I wasn't smarter about the basics or the ease of simple cooking. With very little effort, I could have stocked my kitchen the way I do now and taken much better care of myself.

I'm wiser today. You can see that in my kitchen. In a real, hands-on, visible way, it's a portrait of how much I've grown and where my life is right now. Look at this: various blends of olive oil on the counter next to a cabinet full of spices. Just outside the door, I grow my own basil and rosemary. I also have a couple of tomato plants and some fruit trees. I get pleasure from watching all of these grow, bringing them inside (my version of a harvest), and using them.

Can a kitchen inspire? I believe it can. And I like it when the late afternoon sun streams in through the windows, as it's doing right now, the light pointing to the natural goodies Mother Nature has provided. It's one of life's simple pleasures.

BREAKFAST FAJITAS

YIELD

Serves 2–4

4 flour tortillas (8" diameter)

½ teaspoon olive oil

1 red bell pepper, cored, seeded, and sliced into ½" strips

1 yellow onion, sliced into ½"-thick half moons

1 cup sliced grilled chicken

1½ teaspoons Fajita Spice Mix (opposite page) or packaged seasoning mix

4 egg whites, whisked together

½–1 cup Dominic's Salsa (page 32)

Hot sauce (optional)

Fat-free sour cream (optional)

I have Jenny Craig to thank for inspiring me to make a dish that I once considered strictly Mexican restaurant food. With all of those moving parts that come when you order it—the searing hot skillet, the warm tortillas, the salsa and sour cream—well, I just didn't see myself pulling it all together at my own dinner table. And I have Tom to thank for taking the fajita from dinner to breakfast: He made them for us one morning with leftover grilled chicken from the night before.

This makes a great low-calorie brunch dish. It serves four with delicate appetites or two ravenous ones. Use low-fat whole wheat tortillas, if desired. You can substitute 2 cups of frozen red pepper and onion medley for the fresh, if time is tight. If you don't have time to make your own fajita seasoning, look for Tony Chachere's Original Creole Seasoning, my favorite. If, like me, you can't eat eggs without hot sauce, go for Crystal Hot Sauce or Tabasco Chipotle Pepper Sauce.

PREHEAT THE OVEN to 200°F and arrange the tortillas in a single layer on the oven racks to warm them.

In a small well-seasoned cast-iron or nonstick skillet, heat the oil over medium-low heat. Sprinkle a few droplets of water into the pan. If they sizzle and evaporate, the skillet is hot enough. Add the bell pepper and onion and sauté until soft and fragrant, about 8 minutes. (If using a frozen pepper and onion medley, add to the pan and sauté until thawed and just warmed through.) Add the chicken and seasoning, and continue to sauté until fragrant and the vegetables are thoroughly warmed through.

Add the egg whites to the skillet. As they begin to solidify, use a rubber spatula to move the eggs around the pan to mix with the vegetables and chicken so that the liquid parts are exposed to the heat. When all is cooked through, serve straight from the skillet, spooning the mixture onto the warmed tortillas. Serve with the salsa or hot sauce (if using), and the sour cream (if using) on the side.

Fajita Spice Mix

Making this mix at home allows you to customize it to your liking. I like a bit of heat, so I tend to add even more cayenne than is called for here. Don't limit yourself to sprinkling this on fajitas—just a pinch perks up scrambled eggs, deviled eggs, and chicken salad.

COMBINE THE CHILI powder, cumin, garlic powder, onion powder, brown sugar, paprika, cayenne, salt, cornmeal, and black pepper in a small bowl and whisk together. Store in a small jar with a tight-fitting lid. The mix will keep up to 2 months.

Per serving (when serving 2): *377 calories, 29 g protein, 44 g carbohydrates, 8 g total fat, 1 g saturated fat, 4 g fiber, 966 mg sodium*

Per serving (when serving 4): *188 calories, 15 g protein, 22 g carbohydrates, 4 g total fat, 0.5 g saturated fat, 2 g fiber, 483 mg sodium*

YIELD
Makes about $\frac{1}{4}$ cup

2 tablespoons chili powder

2 teaspoons ground cumin

2 teaspoons garlic powder

1 teaspoon onion powder

1 teaspoon brown sugar

1 teaspoon paprika

$\frac{1}{2}$ teaspoon cayenne

$\frac{1}{2}$ teaspoon kosher salt

$\frac{1}{4}$ teaspoon cornmeal

Freshly ground black pepper

BREAKFAST QUINOA

YIELD

Serves 2

½ cup quinoa, rinsed

1 tablespoon grated fresh ginger

¼ teaspoon nutmeg

Pinch kosher salt

⅓ cup dried cranberries

¼ cup vanilla rice milk

2 tablespoons chopped walnuts, toasted (page 100)

Dr. Oz inspired me to eat quinoa for breakfast, but I would just as easily eat this for lunch or dessert. When I get tired of eating eggs and want something slightly sweet yet healthy, this is what I make. You can add whatever fresh fruit is in season and swap out the dried cranberries for any dried fruit—chopped dates, raisins, or apricots.

COMBINE THE QUINOA with 1 cup water, the ginger, nutmeg, and salt in a small saucepan, and stir until thoroughly combined. Bring to a boil over high heat. Reduce the heat and simmer, covered, 10 minutes.

Stir in the cranberries and the rice milk. Cover and cook, until the water is absorbed and the quinoa is tender, about 5 minutes. Just before serving, stir in the walnuts. Serve warm.

Per serving: *294 calories, 8 g protein, 50 g carbohydrates, 8 g total fat, 1 g saturated fat, 5 g fiber, 93 mg sodium*

BANANA-WALNUT BRAN MUFFINS

½ cup all-purpose flour

½ cup whole wheat flour

½ teaspoon baking powder

½ teaspoon baking soda

¼ teaspoon kosher salt

½ cup (1 stick) unsalted butter, softened

¼ cup packed light brown sugar

2½ ripe bananas, mashed with a fork

2 large eggs

1 teaspoon vanilla extract

½ cup chopped walnuts, toasted (page 100)

2 tablespoons wheat bran

This is another one of those "waste not, want not" recipes (like Challah French Toast, page 5), only this one makes great use of bananas that are beyond their prime eating stage. I found myself making this on many days when Wolfie was in school, because the bananas I bought for his lunch would inevitably become overripe, perfect for muffins. Sometimes I would buy a good-quality bran muffin mix—one with low sodium—and mash the bananas into it, but the truth is, making these from scratch is easier than going out to the store. These never lasted long after I made them, but they can be stored in a container with a tight-fitting lid for up to 2 days. You can also bake the batter into a loaf: Increase both flours by 2 tablespoons and bake in a greased 8½" x 4½" x 2½" loaf pan at 375°F until the bread springs back when pressed, about 45 minutes.

PREHEAT THE OVEN to 350°F. Line 12 cups of a muffin tin with paper liners.

In a medium bowl, whisk together the all-purpose and whole wheat flours, baking powder, baking soda, and salt. In a large bowl, beat the butter and brown sugar together with an electric mixer on high until light and fluffy, about 7 minutes. Add the bananas, eggs, and vanilla, and beat until combined. The batter will look curdled. With the mixer on low, beat the flour mixture into the banana mixture until just combined. Fold in the walnuts.

Divide the batter evenly among the muffin cups. Sprinkle the bran generously over each. Bake 20 minutes, or until a toothpick inserted in the center of a muffin comes out clean. Transfer the pan to a cooling rack and let sit for 10 minutes.

Per muffin: *190 calories, 3 g protein, 19 g carbohydrates, 12 g total fat, 5 g saturated fat, 2 g fiber, 134 mg sodium*

BLUEBERRY YOGURT SMOOTHIE

I prefer using frozen blueberries for this because they give the smoothie a great texture. My trainer insists I use a whey protein and suggests that women never add more than 20 grams of it per drink.

YIELD
Serves 1

½ cup fresh or frozen blueberries

1 cup nonfat vanilla yogurt

1 tablespoon ground flaxseed

1 tablespoon protein powder

COMBINE THE BLUEBERRIES, yogurt, flaxseed, and protein powder in a blender. Add ½ cup ice cubes if using fresh blueberries, and puree until smooth. Pour into a tall glass and enjoy.

Per serving: *342 calories, 23 g protein, 54 g carbohydrates, 5 g total fat, 0.5 g saturated fat, 4 g fiber, 181 mg sodium*

Appetizers
AND Cocktails

They should look special,
and taste even better.

WHEN I WAS little, my dad used to have his friends over for poker nights and my mom made appetizers for them. I recall watching her prepare these bite-size snacks as I leaned against the kitchen counter, impressed that she knew how to make such things. Some looked like three-course meals piled on a single cracker. As I began to prepare this book, I called her and asked, "Mom, do you remember the appetizers you used to make for Daddy's poker nights?" She replied, "Daddy had poker nights?"

I tried to refresh her memory. I described her working in the kitchen as she cooked for his buddies while I fixed them drinks and ferried them into the den. "Really, honey?" she asked. I couldn't believe she didn't remember making rumaki. I could see her hands molding little chicken livers, slicing water chestnuts, pressing them together, and wrapping them in bacon, and then sliding them under the broiler. The kitchen filled with the rich aroma, and my mouth watered, as it did while I reminded my mother of those savory treats. "Don't you remember?" I asked again.

"Oh yes, I made those," she said finally. "But they weren't a big deal."

That's the point of appetizers. Even the most effortless among them should look special, taste even better, and promise the meal ahead will be special. They also create time for relaxed conversation, a rare commodity in this tweet-and-text-driven world.

When I was a child, we played outside before dinner. My parents would talk to each other or friends if they had people over on the weekend. Then my mom would slip back into the kitchen, leaving us to nibble on delicious finger foods until she called us to the table. Now, I do the same thing. At family get-togethers, we'll play touch football or volleyball before dinner, and then I'll set out some appetizers while I put the finishing touches on our meal.

I like my appetizers to be simple. Preparation should be fuss free. There's nothing like chopped-up vegetables—it can't get any easier or healthier. But I've also included a couple of dips, some bacon-wrapped snacks, Italian finger sandwiches, and deviled eggs. Don't be shocked. I know they pack some calories and fat. But hey, these are favorites of mine. I have been making and eating them for years, some since I was a child. They're treats. Everything in moderation.

Likewise the alcoholic libations you'll find in this section. My parents served cocktails alongside appetizers, and I guess I am continuing the tradition. Tom and I are always experimenting with drinks. He likes a great Manhattan. Hence the "summer" Manhattan I suggest.

And I'm gung ho about making my own limoncello.

The appetizers here don't have to be served as starters; they could be the main meal. Like me, more of my friends are going to restaurants and just ordering a few smaller plates off the left side of the menu and calling that a meal. Why not do the same at home? I made sure to include a couple of appetizers that could easily serve as a satisfying lunch or dinner on their own or be combined with a salad or side from one of the other chapters in this book. Tom and I will do this occasionally, and I often eat this way when he is out of town. It's an easy way to control portions. It's also fun, and that, my friends, is what a good appetizer is all about.

ITALIAN FINGER SANDWICHES

Picture this: A handful of burly guys sitting around a table playing poker and eating . . . tea sandwiches. My mother, who is English/Irish, couldn't help herself when it came to making finger food for my dad's poker nights. She took the best of both the English and Italian worlds to turn out these hybrids—top-quality Italian meats, classic Italian dressing, and Italian bread thinly sliced and spread with cream cheese or butter.

STIR TOGETHER THE oil, vinegar, oregano, salt, and pepper in a small bowl. On a work surface, spread out all the bread slices. Brush the oil and vinegar mixture onto half of the bread slices. Spread the remaining slices with softened butter or cream cheese.

Layer the oil-slicked bread slices with these combinations: prosciutto with red peppers, salami with cucumber, and mortadella with pepperoncini. Top each with the buttered bread slices. Using a serrated knife, cut away the crusts from each sandwich. Halve or quarter each sandwich. Place them on a tray and cover with clean, damp kitchen towels to keep them moist until ready to serve.

Per serving: *266 calories, 10 g protein, 18 g carbohydrates, 17 g total fat, 6 g saturated fat, 1 g fiber, 967 mg sodium*

YIELD
Makes about 24 tiny sandwich halves or 48 quartered sandwiches / Serves 12

¼ cup extra-virgin olive oil

2 tablespoons red wine vinegar

½ teaspoon dried oregano

½ teaspoon kosher salt

Freshly ground black pepper

1 loaf (14–16 ounces) Italian bread (from a bakery), sliced into 24 thin, round slices

¼ cup softened butter or cream cheese

⅓ pound thinly sliced prosciutto di Parma

⅓ cup roasted red peppers

⅓ pound thinly sliced salami

½ cucumber, peeled if waxy, thinly sliced

⅓ pound thinly sliced mortadella

4–5 pickled pepperoncini, sliced

DOMINIC'S SALSA

My stepson Dominic's eyes light up when I say I'm making salsa. It seems to disappear before my eyes, and since it requires a bit of chopping, I tend to make it only in big batches, so feel free to double the recipe. If you don't have a Dominic in your house, this salsa will probably keep for a week in the fridge, but I can't be sure because it's never lasted past a day or two in our house! Salsa is an ideal condiment in my book—super flavorful and healthy. If you want a slightly spicier version, use a serrano chile in place of the jalapeño. I love a chunky salsa, but if you like yours smooth and creamy, whirl half the batch (before adding the cilantro) in the blender. There may seem to be an excess of scallions here, but that's just the way Dominic likes it.

YIELD
Makes about 2 cups / Serves 8

5–6 Roma tomatoes, diced

8–10 scallions, chopped to just past where they turn green

½ jalapeño chile pepper, seeds removed and finely chopped (wear plastic gloves when handling)

1–2 cloves garlic, finely chopped to almost a paste

1 cup loosely packed fresh cilantro leaves, chopped

Juice of 1–2 limes

2 teaspoons red wine vinegar

½ teaspoon kosher salt

½ teaspoon ground white pepper

COMBINE THE TOMATOES, scallions, chile pepper (to taste), garlic, cilantro, lime juice (to taste), and red wine vinegar in a medium serving bowl. Add the salt and pepper. Stir to combine. Let sit at room temperature for 10 minutes, stir again, and serve. The salsa can be stored in the refrigerator in a jar with a tight-fitting lid up to a week.

Per serving (¼ cup): *16 calories, 1 g protein, 4 g carbohydrates, 0 g total fat, 0 g saturated fat, 1 g fiber, 126 mg sodium*

Cajun Cream Cheese Dip

My go-to dip is generally hummus, but when I want something a bit spicier, I go for this easy mix of Neufchâtel and fajita spices, either homemade or Tony Chachere's Original Creole Seasoning. Serve this with sliced radishes, cucumbers, whole grape tomatoes, and fennel cut into thin half moons.

COMBINE THE CREAM cheese, spice mix, lemon juice, and hot sauce (to taste) in a small bowl and stir until the ingredients are thoroughly combined. Taste and adjust the seasonings. Serve with your favorite dipping vegetables.

Per serving: 74 calories, 3 g protein, 2 g carbohydrates, 7 g total fat, 4 g saturated fat, 0 g fiber, 140 mg sodium

◤ YIELD
Makes about 1 cup / Serves 8

8 ounces Neufchâtel cheese or other reduced-fat cream cheese, softened

1 tablespoon Fajita Spice Mix (page 17) or store-bought Creole seasoning

Juice of ½ lemon

Hot sauce, such as Crystal Hot Sauce or Tabasco Chipotle Pepper Sauce

CREAM CHEESE CRAB SPREAD

YIELD

Makes 1 (8") log / Serves 18

8 ounces Neufchâtel cheese or other reduced-fat cream cheese, softened

1 pound fresh crabmeat, picked over for shells

4 tablespoons ketchup

4 tablespoons prepared horseradish

Juice of ½ lemon

1 teaspoon kosher salt

Freshly ground black pepper

½ cup chopped fresh chives (optional)

Crackers

This was the first recipe I asked my mother for when I moved away from home. It was her instant cocktail party dish—and one all of her friends raved about. Call it old-fashioned, but I guarantee every last bit of it will vanish within minutes of setting it out. Add the chopped chives if you want to fancy it up, but she never did!

COMBINE THE CREAM cheese and all but ½ cup of the crabmeat in a medium bowl. Mix until thoroughly combined. Roll into an 8" log and refrigerate until firmed up slightly, about 1 hour.

Meanwhile, combine the ketchup, horseradish, lemon juice, salt, and pepper in a medium bowl. Taste and adjust to your liking.

Place the log on a serving platter. Spoon the sauce all over it. Sprinkle the reserved crabmeat on top and garnish with the chives, if using. Serve with your favorite crackers.

Per serving (without crackers): *61 calories, 7 g protein, 2 g carbohydrates, 3 g total fat, 2 g saturated fat, 0 g fiber, 288 mg sodium*

Prosciutto Bruschetta

YIELD
Serves 8

8 slices crusty sourdough bread, cut on the diagonal from a 1-pound loaf

Extra-virgin olive oil

1 clove garlic

8 thinly sliced fresh mozzarella

8 thinly sliced prosciutto

8 leaves fresh basil

The weekend that I met Tom, we ended up in the kitchen cooking together, and it felt remarkably comfortable—I mean really comfortable. We were in charge of the appetizers, and my brother and his wife were in charge of dinner. Luckily, a few weekends before, I had been at my friend Suzanne's and she made these, which made me look like a very good impromptu cook in front of Tom. Use only fresh mozzarella (packed in water). And be sure the bread is brushed all over with the olive oil, or else it will have unappetizing dry spots.

PREHEAT THE BROILER. Brush the bread on both sides generously with oil and place on a baking sheet. Broil until golden and crisp, 2 minutes per side.

Remove, let cool slightly, and rub the garlic all over one side of each slice. Place a slice of cheese on each piece of bread, then top each with a slice of prosciutto. Return to the oven until the cheese is melted and golden, about 2 minutes.

Garnish with a basil leaf and serve.

Per serving: *258 calories, 14 g protein, 33 g carbohydrates, 9 g total fat, 3 g saturated fat, 1 g fiber, 684 mg sodium*

SUMMER BRUSCHETTA

If you saw the movie *Julie and Julia*, you'll remember one of the opening scenes when Julie was making bruschetta for herself and her husband. The camera so evocatively captured just how seductive this simple, rustic Italian snack can be. Go heavy on the garlic if you don't have to kiss anyone (unless that someone is eating this with you) or light if you want to attract vampires. Me? I *loooooove* me some garlic! Don't bother making this with anything but fresh tomatoes from the farm stand. The black olives are meant to subtly flavor the mix; use too many and they'll overwhelm the whole thing. You can replace the olives with capers without losing that essential salty flavor.

COMBINE THE CHOPPED garlic, tomatoes, basil, olives, vinegar, and 1 tablespoon of the olive oil in a bowl. Season to taste with salt and pepper. Stir to combine the ingredients and set aside at room temperature to allow the flavors to meld.

Preheat the broiler. Brush the bread on both sides generously with oil and place on a baking sheet. Broil until golden and crisp, 2 minutes per side. Rub one side of each slice with the remaining garlic clove.

Arrange the bread slices, garlic-rubbed side up, on a platter and spoon a heaping tablespoon of the tomato mixture over each piece. Serve immediately.

Per serving: *238 calories, 8 g protein, 41 g carbohydrates, 5 g total fat, 1 g saturated fat, 2 g fiber, 535 mg sodium*

YIELD
Serves 8

3–6 fat cloves garlic, all but one finely chopped

2 cups chopped tomatoes, with their seeds and juice

10 leaves fresh basil, cut into thin strips

10–12 kalamata olives (about 1 ounce), pitted and quartered

1 tablespoon balsamic vinegar

1 tablespoon extra-virgin olive oil plus additional for brushing the bread slices

Kosher salt and freshly ground black pepper

One 1-pound baguette, sliced on the diagonal into 12–16 rounds

PUREED ARTICHOKE CROSTINI

This super-easy appetizer—it's essentially one of those toss-it-all-in-the-food-processor spreads—is based on a Jenny Craig recipe that I love. Rather than make the artichokes the base, as she did, I pureed them with the cheeses and spinach, then spread the mixture on crostini.

HEAT THE OIL in a medium sauté pan over medium heat. Add the artichokes, spinach, pressed garlic, and 1 teaspoon of the lemon juice and sauté until the spinach begins to wilt and the garlic becomes fragrant, about 10 minutes. Remove from the heat and transfer to a food processor. Add the Parmigiano-Reggiano, feta, parsley, and the remaining 2 tablespoons lemon juice and pulse until smooth. Add the salt and season to taste with pepper.

Rub the whole garlic clove onto one side of each slice of bread. Divide the artichoke mixture equally among the slices. Place on a platter and serve, or spoon into a serving bowl and serve with the bread slices. Garnish the platter with the asparagus spears and radishes.

Per serving: *253 calories, 13 g protein, 43 g carbohydrates, 4 g total fat, 2 g saturated fat, 2 g fiber, 745 mg sodium*

YIELD
Makes 16 / Serves 8

2 teaspoons olive oil

12 ounces artichoke hearts, frozen or jarred in water

1⅓ cups baby spinach

3 cloves garlic, 1 left whole, 2 pushed through a press

2 tablespoons plus 1 teaspoon freshly squeezed lemon juice

¼ cup grated Parmigiano-Reggiano cheese

3 tablespoons crumbled feta cheese

2 tablespoons fresh flat-leaf parsley leaves

¼ teaspoon kosher salt

Freshly ground black pepper

One 1-pound baguette, sliced into 16 rounds and toasted

Asparagus spears and radishes for garnish

Indulgent? Sometimes

I UNDERSTAND THAT MANY of the recipes in this book are decadent and not what you would find in a diet book. While I am a proponent of moderation and the occasional splurge, I was not too long ago extremely strict about controlling what and how much I ate, and about making sure that I exercised daily. It's no secret that I relied on Jenny Craig to help me relearn how to eat and enjoy food, how to change my whole approach to mealtimes, and how to refashion a healthier lifestyle. Jenny always emphasizes that it's not about deprivation. It's about eating proper amounts of food, which she insists should be delicious. So I am including recipes for some of the appetizers that she's given me, including this one, along with Jenny's Steak Towers (page 48) Lime Shrimp Skewers (page 42), and Pureed Artichoke Crostini (page 39). The bottom line is I can be good to myself and still enjoy delicious, flavorful food. So can you.

STUFFED MUSHROOMS

This is a traditionally calorie-laden appetizer, rethought by Jenny Craig and beloved by me.

YIELD
Makes 12 / Serves 6

PREHEAT THE OVEN to 325°F. Brush a baking sheet with 1 teaspoon of the oil.

Finely chop the mushroom stems and set aside. Place the mushroom caps on the baking sheet and bake 12 minutes.

Meanwhile, heat the remaining 1 teaspoon oil in a medium skillet over medium heat. Add the mushroom stems, spinach, onion, and garlic and sauté until the spinach wilts, about 6 minutes. Add the tomatoes and cook 2 minutes more. Turn off the heat and stir in the parsley and salt.

Preheat the broiler. Divide the spinach mixture evenly among the mushroom caps. Sprinkle each with the cheese and panko, then broil until golden brown, 2 to 3 minutes. Serve warm.

Per serving: *35 calories, 1 g protein, 3 g carbohydrates, 2 g total fat, 0 g saturated fat, 0.5 g fiber, 123 mg sodium*

2 teaspoons extra-virgin olive oil

12 large white mushrooms, brushed clean and stems removed and reserved

½ cup baby spinach, finely chopped

½ onion, minced

2 cloves garlic, pushed through a press

½ cup finely chopped cherry tomatoes

2 tablespoons chopped fresh flat-leaf parsley

⅛ teaspoon salt plus additional for sprinkling on mushroom caps

Freshly ground black pepper

1 tablespoon grated Pecorino Romano cheese

1 tablespoon panko bread crumbs

LIME SHRIMP SKEWERS

YIELD

Makes 16 / Serves 8

1 tablespoon olive oil

1 small onion, thinly sliced

⅓ cup tequila

¼ cup freshly squeezed lime juice

¼ cup fresh cilantro leaves, chopped

3 cloves garlic, pushed through a press

¼ teaspoon cayenne

½ teaspoon kosher salt

1 pound small shrimp, peeled and deveined

1 red bell pepper, cut into 1" squares

1 yellow bell pepper, cut into 1" squares

1 orange bell pepper, cut into 1" squares

16 small mushrooms

Lime wedges

This is based on a Jenny Craig recipe that will always remain in my repertoire. Marinating the shrimp for at least an hour is the secret to these juicy grilled morsels.

SOAK 16 WOODEN or bamboo skewers in water for 20 minutes (snip them if they're longer than 6").

Combine the oil, onion, tequila, lime juice, cilantro, garlic, cayenne, and salt in a large bowl and mix well. Place the shrimp, peppers, and mushrooms in the marinade and stir. Refrigerate for 1 hour, stirring once.

Assemble the skewers by threading the ingredients onto them in this order: bell pepper, shrimp, mushroom, pepper, shrimp, and pepper. Reserve the marinade.

Coat a grill rack with oil and preheat the grill on high for 5 minutes. Turn the heat to medium-high and cook the skewers, covered, 6 minutes, flipping and then basting them with the marinade once halfway through the cooking. Discard the remaining marinade. Serve with wedges of lime to squeeze over the skewers before eating.

Per serving: *120 calories, 13 g protein, 6 g carbohydrates, 3 g total fat, 0 g saturated fat, 1 g fiber, 240 mg sodium*

RUMAKI TERIYAKI

Bacon. Give me anything with bacon! These may seem old-fashioned, but my feeling is, whenever I can make something that's a vehicle for bacon, I will. I was reminded of these when my favorite market near my house made bacon-wrapped dates for tasting. It brought back memories of the rumaki my mom used to make for my dad's poker parties. Decades later, it hasn't lost its appeal.

YIELD
Makes 24 / Serves 12

¼ pound chicken livers, trimmed and rinsed

⅓ cup teriyaki sauce plus additional for basting

1 clove garlic, pushed through a press

12 canned water chestnuts, drained and halved

12 slices low-sodium bacon, halved crosswise

CUT THE CHICKEN livers into 24 roughly ½" pieces. Stir together the teriyaki sauce and garlic in a medium bowl, then add the livers and water chestnuts. Toss to coat. Marinate, covered, in the refrigerator for at least 1 hour. Soak 28 toothpicks in cold water for 1 hour.

Preheat the broiler. Remove the livers and water chestnuts from the marinade and discard the marinade. Lay 1 bacon half on a cutting board and place 1 piece of liver and 1 water chestnut in the center. Fold one side of the bacon over them, and thread a toothpick through the bacon, then the chestnut and liver. Wrap the remaining bacon edge around this parcel and secure on the toothpick. Repeat with remaining ingredients to make 24 rumaki.

Broil the rumaki on the rack of a broiler pan 2" from the heat about 4 minutes. Flip them over and broil 2 minutes more. Brush the rumaki with additional teriyaki sauce and return to the broiler for 2 more minutes. Place on a serving tray and serve immediately.

Per serving: 97 calories, 8 g protein, 4 g carbohydrates, 5 g total fat, 3 g saturated fat, 0 g fiber, 315 mg sodium

T's Bacon-Wrapped Shrimp in Creamy Horseradish Sauce

YIELD
Makes 24 / Serves 12

Here's Tom's version of that cocktail party classic, bacon-wrapped shrimp. It may seem a little retro, but I guarantee that these will be the first thing guests go for—and they'll want more. The sauce is pretty rich, so I thoroughly enjoy just one but plan for two for each of my guests. This was one of the first dishes we cooked together (along with the Prosciutto Bruschetta on page 36) after we met. (Love at first bite? Okay, okay . . . sorry, I'm corny!) Ask your fish guy to devein the peeled shrimp for you. It makes assembling these much faster.

24 extra-large shrimp, peeled and deveined

24 canned water chestnuts, drained, (one 8-ounce can)

12 slices bacon, halved crosswise

6 tablespoons (¾ stick) unsalted butter

1 package (8 ounces) cream cheese, softened

½ cup mayonnaise

½ cup sour cream

3 tablespoons prepared horseradish

1 tablespoon freshly squeezed lemon juice

Tabasco sauce

Kosher salt and ground white pepper

WRAP 1 SHRIMP around 1 water chestnut. Wrap a piece of bacon around the whole thing and secure with a toothpick. Repeat with the remaining shrimp, water chestnuts, and bacon.

Melt 3 tablespoons of the butter in a large heavy skillet over medium-high heat. Add half of the shrimp and cook, turning, until the bacon browns, about 2½ minutes per side. Transfer to a large gratin dish, and repeat with the remaining butter and shrimp.

Preheat the broiler. Put the cream cheese in a medium bowl and beat until smooth. Add the mayonnaise, sour cream, horseradish, lemon juice, and Tabasco, salt, and pepper to taste. Beat until blended. Taste and adjust the seasonings. Spoon the sauce over the shrimp. Broil until the top is golden brown, 1 to 2 minutes. Serve warm, straight from the dish.

Per serving: *336 calories, 7 g protein, 6 g carbohydrates, 32 g total fat, 13 g saturated fat, 1 g fiber, 364 mg sodium*

Kale Chips, Three Ways

YIELD
Makes about 3 cups / Serves 6

6 cups tightly packed kale leaves (from 1 bunch), center stems and any other thick ribs removed, each torn into several pieces

1–2 tablespoons olive oil

Kosher salt and freshly ground black pepper

Cindy and Deb, who both work on the set of *Hot in Cleveland*, invariably show up with a big batch of these. And thank God for that! Each has her own version: Deb's are loaded with cheese, seasonings, and pine nuts; Cindy's are deliciously straightforward. Deb uses a dehydrator, and Cindy uses an oven. The leafy greens—which are loaded with calcium and beta-carotene—are completely addictive when you toss them in a little olive oil and bake them. The key is to totally coat every kale leaf, so my method is to put the kale in a 2-gallon resealable plastic bag, pour in the oil, and then shake and massage the bag so you can see what still needs coating. The baking time will vary, depending on how curly the kale leaves are. Be sure to allow them to cool completely before piling into a bowl or sealing in a container.

Classic

PREHEAT THE OVEN to 300°F. Place the kale in a 2-gallon resealable plastic bag. Add the oil and shake and massage the kale to coat each piece entirely. Season with salt and pepper and shake again.

Spread the kale in a single layer on 2 large baking sheets. Bake until the leaves become crispy, 22 to 26 minutes. If any leaves remain flexible (as opposed to a crisp crunch), return them to the oven for 2 minutes more. Allow to cool completely before transfering to a serving bowl or storage container.

Per serving: *60 calories, 2 g protein, 7 g carbohydrates, 4 g total fat, 0.5 g saturated fat, 1 g fiber, 55 mg sodium*

Italian-Style

IMMEDIATELY AFTER REMOVING the kale from the oven, toss the leaves with the cheese and pine nuts until evenly incorporated throughout. Serve immediately.

$\frac{1}{4}$ cup grated Parmigiano-Reggiano or Pecorino Romano cheese

$\frac{1}{4}$ cup pine nuts, toasted (page 100)

Per serving: *116 calories, 4 g protein, 8 g carbohydrates, 9 g total fat, 1 g saturated fat, 2 g fiber, 106 mg sodium*

Seaside Spice

AFTER SEASONING THE kale with the salt and pepper, add the Old Bay Seasoning and cayenne to the bag and massage into the leaves. Immediately after removing the kale from the oven, toss with the lemon zest.

1 teaspoon Old Bay Seasoning

$\frac{1}{8}$ teaspoon cayenne

Zest of 1 lemon, grated

Per serving: *64 calories, 2 g protein, 7 g carbohydrates, 4 g total fat, 0.5 g saturated fat, 1 g fiber, 161 mg sodium*

Jenny's Steak Towers

YIELD

Makes about 24 / Serves 12

8 ounces beef tenderloin steak or filet mignon

Kosher salt and freshly ground black pepper

3 ounces Neufchâtel cheese or other reduced-fat cream cheese, softened

1 teaspoon freshly squeezed lemon juice

¼ teaspoon sugar

1 tablespoon chopped fresh basil, mint, or flat-leaf parsley

½ English cucumber, sliced into ¼"-thick rounds

2 tablespoons thinly sliced grape or cherry tomatoes

2 tablespoons finely chopped red onion

Who doesn't love the sound of a steak tower? Thank God Jenny Craig is there when I want something decadent but know I shouldn't. The key is to eat something super flavorful—in small quantities—like these great appetizers.

COAT A GRILL rack with oil and preheat the grill on high heat for 5 minutes. Meanwhile, season the beef all over with salt and pepper. Reduce the heat to medium-high and grill the steak over direct heat with the cover closed, turning once, until medium rare, about 10 minutes. Transfer to a cutting board and let rest for 5 minutes, then cut into ½"-thick slices. Cut the slices into 1" squares.

Combine the cream cheese, lemon juice, sugar, and basil in a small bowl, and mix until thoroughly combined. Spoon the mixture into a resealable plastic bag with one corner snipped.

To assemble, place a square of steak on top of a cucumber slice, then pipe a teaspoon of the cream cheese mixture on top. Repeat with the remaining steak and cucumber slices. Garnish each with the basil, tomatoes, and onion and serve.

Per serving: *51 calories, 5 g protein, 1 g carbohydrates, 3 g total fat, 1.5 g saturated fat, 0 g fiber, 70 mg sodium*

DEVILED EGGS, THREE WAYS

I love a well-prepared egg—scrambled, poached, Scotched, and especially deviled. I can't imagine a summer without deviled eggs. My mother used to make them as a rule for summer parties, the classic version sprinkled with paprika and chopped chives. But there are endless possibilities. I've given three of my favorites here, but feel free to use your imagination.

YIELD
Makes 24 / Serves 12

12 large eggs, in their shells
Greens for lining the serving platter

TO HARD-BOIL EGGS: Fill a large, deep saucepan with a tight-fitting lid with 2" of cold water. Place the eggs in it and bring to a boil over medium-high heat. Immediately turn off the heat and cover with the lid. Let sit for 12 minutes. Transfer to a colander and rinse under cold water. Once cooled, peel.

Slice in half, lengthwise. Scoop out the yolks and place 4 yolks in each of three bowls. Mash well with a fork. Line a large serving platter with the greens. Mash one of the following into each bowl:

PICKLES AND CAPERS

ADD THE GHERKINS. mustard, and mayonnaise to the yolks and mash together until thoroughly incorporated. Season to taste with salt and pepper. Divide the filling among 8 egg halves. Top each with the capers and place on the platter.

2 sweet gherkins, finely chopped
2 teaspoons spicy brown mustard
2 tablespoons mayonnaise
Kosher salt and freshly ground
   black pepper
Capers

Per egg half: *106 calories, 6 g protein, 4 g carbohydrates, 7 g total fat, 2 g saturated fat, 0 g fiber, 225 mg sodium*

(continued)

Wasabi and Ginger

1 tablespoon prepared wasabi

¼ cucumber, peeled if waxy and finely chopped

2 tablespoons mayonnaise

Kosher salt and freshly ground black pepper

Pickled ginger

ADD THE WASABI, cucumber, and mayonnaise to the yolks and mash together. Season to taste with salt and pepper. Divide the filling among 8 egg halves. Top each with a slice of pickled ginger and place on the platter.

Per egg half: *66 calories, 3 g protein, 1 g carbohydrates, 5 g total fat, 1 g saturated fat, 0 g fiber, 77 mg sodium*

Sesame Cilantro

½ small carrot, finely chopped

1 tablespoon mayonnaise

2 teaspoons sesame oil

1 teaspoon toasted sesame seeds

Kosher salt and freshly ground black pepper

8 leaves fresh cilantro

ADD THE CARROT, mayonnaise, oil, and sesame seeds to the yolks and mash together. Season to taste with salt and pepper. Divide the filling among 8 egg halves. Top each with a cilantro leaf and place on the platter.

Per egg half: *27 calories, 0 g protein, 0.5 g carbohydrates, 2.5 g total fat, 0.5 g saturated fat, 0 g fiber, 28 mg sodium*

SERIOUSLY GOOD SAUSAGE BITES

So simple, so tasty! This recipe instantly brings me back to the kitchen of my childhood and the memory of my parents working together, in perfect sync, in the kitchen. On dad's poker nights, he kneaded the ingredients together, and mom would form the balls and pop 'em in the oven. Then they would clean up the mess together. It could be that these appetizers are directly responsible for my only wanting a man who is comfortable in the kitchen.

PREHEAT THE OVEN to 400°F and arrange the racks in the upper and lower third of the oven. Coat 2 baking sheets with the cooking spray.

Cook the sausage in a medium skillet over medium high heat, breaking it up with a wooden spoon, until cooked through and no pink remains. Using a slotted spoon, transfer the sausage to a paper towel-lined plate and set aside.

Combine the flour and butter in a food processor and pulse until the mixture resembles coarse meal with some larger chunks of butter remaining. Drizzle in the buttermilk and Tabasco and pulse just until the dough comes together. Turn the dough out into a large bowl and fold in the sausage and cheese. Using two spoons, shape the dough into walnut-size balls and drop onto the baking sheets.

Bake, switching and rotating the pans halfway through baking, until golden and cooked through, about 15 minutes. Let cool on the baking sheets for 5 minutes, then use a spatula to remove and transfer to a platter. Bake the remaining sausage bites in the same manner.

Per serving: 190 calories, 6 g protein, 15 g carbohydrates, 11 g total fat, 6 g saturated fat, 1 g fiber, 435 mg sodium

YIELD
Makes about 60 / Serves 20

Cooking spray

10 ounces bulk hot Italian sausage

3 cups self-rising flour

6 tablespoons (¾ stick) unsalted butter

1½ cups buttermilk

1 tablespoon Tabasco sauce

1¼ cups (about 6 ounces) grated sharp Cheddar cheese

LIMONCELLO

Lemons grow like crazy right outside my door, so it stands to reason that I would teach myself how to make this classic southern Italian liqueur. Be sure to use organic lemons; the zest is key to flavoring this refreshing *digestif*.

YIELD

Makes 2 quarts plus 1 cup
(36 2-ounce servings)

14 organic lemons

1 liter vodka

3 cups sugar

Photo on page 56.

GRATE THE ZEST from the lemons using a Microplane grater, taking care to leave the pith behind. Place the zest in a 3-quart pitcher. Pour the vodka over it and stir. Cover with plastic wrap and set in a spot where it won't be disturbed, at room temperature, and let steep 1 week.

Combine 3½ cups water and the sugar in a large saucepan and cook over medium heat until the sugar dissolves, stirring occasionally, about 10 minutes. Let cool completely, then pour the syrup into the pitcher with the zest and stir. Cover tightly again and let stand 24 hours. Strain through a fine-mesh sieve and discard the solids. Pour into clean bottles with tight-fitting caps. Refrigerate until well chilled, at least 4 hours or up to 1 month.

Per serving: *125 calories, 0 g protein, 17 g carbohydrates, 0 g total fat, 0 g saturated fat, 0 g fiber, 1 mg sodium*

(Opposite) *One of the wonderful benefits of living in California: my lemon trees*

(Left) *Limoncello for sale along a hiking trail in Tuscany*

Left to right: *Summer Manhattan (page 61); Lemon Ginger and Rye (page 60); Limoncello (page 55); Italian Spritz (page 59); and Grapefruitini (page 58)*

GRAPEFRUITINI

YIELD
Serves 1

1 thin wedge grapefruit, with peel on, halved

2 tablespoons cocktail rimming sugar, spooned onto a saucer

Ice cubes

Juice of ½ grapefruit

1 shot (1½ ounces) citrus vodka

1 shot (1½ ounces) white cranberry juice

Photo on page 57.

The very shape of a martini glass suggests a special occasion, and when one comes around, I'm drawn to this delicious, pretty drink.

RUN HALF THE wedge of grapefruit around the rim of a martini glass. Dip the martini glass in the sugar to coat the rim. Tap off the excess.

Fill a cocktail shaker with ice. Pour 1 shot (1½ ounces) of the grapefruit juice, the vodka, and cranberry juice into the shaker and shake until well chilled. Strain into the martini glass. Serve immediately.

Per serving: *250 calories, 1 g protein, 39 g carbohydrates, 0 g total fat, 0 g saturated fat, 0 g fiber, 0 mg sodium*

ITALIAN SPRITZ

Yum. I first tasted this lovely drink in Tuscany at the beautiful hotel Borgo San Felice. It was served in a very large red wine glass, poured over ice. Tom likes to add vodka to the mix when he wants what he calls a "real" drink and not a fussy one. For me, the bittersweet Aperol combined with sparkling Prosecco is just right.

FILL A WINE or larger glass with ice. Add the Aperol, Prosecco, and sparkling water and shake until well chilled. Stir and garnish with the fruit. Serve immediately.

Per serving: *354 calories, 0 g protein, 35 g carbohydrates, 0 g total fat, 0 g saturated fat, 1 g fiber, 6 mg sodium*

YIELD
Serves 1

Ice cubes

2 shots (3 ounces) Aperol

2 shots (3 ounces) Prosecco

2 shots (3 ounces) sparkling water

3–4 chunks fruit, such as strawberry, pineapple, lemon, orange, or lime sliced thinly with rind on, and all skewered on a decorative cocktail pick

Photo on page 57.

LEMON GINGER AND RYE

2 thin slices fresh cucumber

2 thin slices fresh lemon

Ice cubes

2 shots (3 ounces) Pimm's #5

3 shots (4½ ounces) ginger beer

2 shots (3 ounces) sparkling water

Photo on page 56.

Whenever Tom and I travel to a major American city—or anywhere for that matter—we invariably research the locale's restaurants first. When in Chicago, we love to go to Art Smith's Table Fifty-Two, where we first tasted a version of this delicious combination.

PLACE THE CUCUMBER and lemon in a highball glass, and using a muddler, mash them lightly to release their juices. Fill the glass with ice cubes and pour the Pimm's, ginger beer, and sparkling water into it. Stir once and serve immediately.

Per serving: *202 calories, 0 g protein, 17 g carbohydrates, 0 g total fat, 0 g saturated fat, 1 g fiber, 8 mg sodium*

SUMMER MANHATTAN

Tom loves a good Manhattan in the winter but skips the classic version in the summer because it's too heavy. Aperol and Prosecco replace rye in this warm-weather version of the traditional cocktail. You can find jars of Luxardo-brand maraschino cherries in specialty gourmet shops or online; in a pinch, use regular maraschinos.

PLACE THE CHERRY in a highball glass and chill in the freezer. Meanwhile, fill a shaker with ice. Add the Aperol, Antica, and bitters and shake well. Strain into the highball glass, add a few ice cubes, and top with the Champagne.

Per serving: *325 calories, 0 g protein, 28 g carbohydrates, 0 g total fat, 0 g saturated fat, 0 g fiber, 4 mg sodium*

YIELD
Serves 1

1 Luxardo cherry

1 shot (1½ ounces) Aperol

1 shot (1½ ounces) Antica sweet vermouth

3 short shakes angostura bitters

3 shots (4½ ounces) Champagne or Prosecco

Photo on page 56.

Soups AND Sandwiches

Relish the hearty aromas
that fill your kitchen.

I KNEW MY HUSBAND was an emotional man, but I didn't realize the extent of it until we were on our honeymoon in Rome. We had a tour guide, and Tom asked him to take us to an out-of-the-way place for lunch. He made only one request: He didn't want to see any tourists. He wanted to go someplace where the food was delicious and known only to locals. So we set off down several streets and a couple of alleys, and finally arrived at a place where our guide knocked on a wooden door. An older woman stepped out and ushered us inside. Tom began to weep. "It smells like my grandmother's house," he said, deeply moved but so happy. Turning to our host, he said, "Bring me anything."

A few minutes later, she brought us three bowls of ribollita, a thick tomato-based vegetable soup with chunks of bread wallowing beneath the surface. Seeing the look on Tom's face, I was glad that I had made our relationship legal before he met this septuagenarian Italian grandma with the great soup. That experience alone convinced me that I had to include a section in this book on soups. He's not the only one in the family, though, who's nuts about soup. When Wolfie was a little boy, I used to take him to a local restaurant after soccer practice, and he always ordered the pasta *e fagioli*. He still does. That provided me

with the excuse to finally learn how to make it.

Like those soups, the recipes in this section are all very personal, maybe more intimate than any others in this book. Every recipe has been culled from a family member or a personal experience—like the pasta *e fagioli*—that led me to want to not only learn how to make it, but also share it. But tuna melt? Come on, who puts tuna melt in their cookbook? Me! I learned to make it in my seventh-grade home economics class.

Tuscan Soup, Jenny Craig–Style (page 69) had to be included here, too. It's low cal and filling, and I can't tell you how many weeks of losing weight it got me through without feeling cheated. And the homemade bread that comes from my Aunt Adeline was the epitome of deliciousness when I was little. Now, when I handle the dough—though somewhat differently than my mother and her mother and her mother did—it's like sifting through the history of the women in my family and connecting with them in a way that I want to believe my great-

great-great grandmother would understand if she saw me in my kitchen today.

That is magical. And that's why, when you try the soups, breads, and sandwiches in this section, I want you to put aside thoughts of calories and carbs and instead relish the hearty aromas that fill your kitchen, the tastes that awaken your tongue, and the smiles that appear around the table.

Pasta e Fagioli

This was Wolfie's favorite meal at Il Tiramisù, the Sherman Oaks restaurant that was long our first stop after soccer practice. He would order a bowl of this and do his homework at the table. And I'd have a glass of wine! When I make it at home, it just never looks or tastes right during any of the cooking phases, but it really comes together at the very last minute. It will look a tiny bit better, but too thin, after pureeing. Then somehow, once you add the noodles—poof!—perfect pasta *e fagioli* from the Old Country.

COMBINE THE ONION, celery, carrot, bay leaf, and oil in a medium saucepan. Cover and cook over medium-low heat 5 minutes. Add the tomatoes with their juices and continue to cook, covered, stirring occasionally, until the vegetables are soft, about 15 minutes. Add the rosemary sprig and broth, cover, and bring to a boil. Reduce the heat and simmer, partially covered, 15 minutes. Add the beans and simmer gently, 5 minutes. Discard the rosemary sprig and bay leaf.

Using an immersion blender, blend most of the soup, leaving it as chunky as desired. Alternatively, puree in batches in a blender. Taste the soup and adjust for seasoning with salt and pepper.

Meanwhile, cook the pasta according to package directions. Set aside 1 cup of the cooking water and drain the pasta. Add the pasta to the soup and use the cooking water to thin the soup, if desired. Ladle into bowls, drizzle each with a little olive oil, and sprinkle with cheese.

Per serving: *206 calories, 8 g protein, 25 g carbohydrates, 8 g total fat, 2 g saturated fat, 6 g fiber, 666 mg sodium*

YIELD
Serves 4

½ yellow onion, finely chopped

1 rib celery, preferably with leaves, finely chopped

1 carrot, finely chopped

1 bay leaf

2 tablespoons extra-virgin olive oil plus additional for drizzling

2 plum tomatoes, diced

1 sprig rosemary

3 cups reduced-sodium chicken broth

1 can (15.5 ounces) Roman beans, cannellini beans, or kidney beans, rinsed and drained

Kosher salt and freshly ground black pepper

1 cup ditalini, elbows, or tripolini pasta

Grated Parmigiano-Reggiano cheese

Caution!

Remove the central plug from the blender lid when blending hot liquids to avoid a hot mini-explosion. Instead, fold a kitchen towel and hold it over the lid while blending.

TURKEY MEATBALL SOUP

YIELD

Serves 10

1 white onion, finely chopped

2 cloves garlic, minced

3 tablespoons extra-virgin olive oil plus additional for sautéing the meatballs

2 ribs celery, preferably with leaves, chopped

2 cartons (32 ounces each) reduced-sodium chicken broth

2 carrots, sliced into ¼" rounds

2 bay leaves

¾ cup Italian-style bread crumbs

½ cup finely grated Parmigiano-Reggiano plus additional for serving

1 pound ground turkey

1 egg

1 cup orzo pasta

2 cups shredded cooked white-meat turkey

1–2 teaspoons dried oregano

Kosher salt and freshly ground black pepper

Call it our chicken soup, but when Wolfie was under the weather, I made this soup for him. In fact, he used to say he wasn't feeling well just to get me to make it. The broth, pasta, and meatballs are in perfect proportion if you serve it immediately, but if it's set aside for even 45 minutes, the pasta tends to take over and the soup becomes more like a stew. If you want it to remain a soup, reheat it and add water by the ¼ cup, tasting and seasoning as you go, until you achieve the desired consistency.

COOK HALF OF the chopped onion and all the garlic in 1 tablespoon of the oil in a large skillet on medium-low heat, stirring occasionally, until soft, about 7 minutes. Transfer to a large bowl and let cool. Wipe the skillet clean.

Cook the celery and remaining onion in the remaining 2 tablespoons oil in a large soup pot, stirring occasionally, until soft, about 8 minutes. Add the broth and increase the heat to high. When it starts to slightly simmer, add the carrots and bay leaves. Keep an eye on the broth, so that it never quite boils.

Meanwhile, to the bowl of cooling onions and garlic, add the bread crumbs, cheese, ground turkey, and egg. Get in there with your bare hands and mix, rolling them into bite-size meatballs. It's more time consuming, but I like them real small.

Pour enough olive oil into the cleaned skillet to just coat the bottom. Working in batches, brown the meatballs over medium heat. As they brown, throw them—gently!—into the broth (you don't want them splashing you). Don't worry about the meatballs being cooked all the way through; the broth will take care of that.

Once all the meatballs have been added, add the orzo and continue to simmer for 15 minutes. Add the shredded turkey and oregano to taste and let it heat up. Turn off the heat and season with salt and pepper. Serve immediately with some cheese sprinkled over each bowl.

Per serving: *262 calories, 20 g protein, 20 g carbohydrates, 11 g total fat, 2.5 g saturated fat, 2 g fiber, 576 mg sodium*

TUSCAN SOUP, JENNY CRAIG–STYLE

Thank you, Jenny, for this incredibly easy, super-satisfying soup. It's a combination that helped this busy working mom shed unwanted pounds without feeling deprived. The eggplant and mushrooms give it nice heft, yet the calorie count is surprisingly low. On the program, you're allowed to sip on this all day, which I did because it didn't seem at all like a diet soup.

COMBINE THE EGGPLANT, tomatoes, mushrooms, squash, broth, garlic, oregano, and pepper in a large soup pot. Set over high heat and bring to a boil. Cover, reduce the heat, and simmer until the vegetables are tender, about 25 minutes. Ladle into soup bowls, sprinkle with some grated cheese, and garnish with the basil.

Per serving: *88 calories, 5 g protein, 13 g carbohydrates, 2 g total fat, 2 g saturated fat, 5 g fiber, 572 mg sodium*

YIELD

Serves 4

1½ cups peeled and cubed eggplant (1 medium)

1 can (14.5 ounces) diced tomatoes

1 cup sliced mushrooms

1 cup chopped yellow squash (about 1 small)

1½ cups (14.5 ounces) reduced-sodium chicken or vegetable broth

1 clove garlic, pushed through a press

½ teaspoon dried oregano

⅛ teaspoon freshly ground black pepper

Pecorino Romano cheese, freshly grated

8 leaves fresh basil, cut into thin strips

MINT CUCUMBER SOUP

YIELD

Serves 4–6

2 English cucumbers

1½ cups plain Greek 0% yogurt

½ cup sour cream

½ clove garlic, pushed through
a press

2 tablespoons torn fresh mint leaves
plus additional for garnish

¾ teaspoon kosher salt

White pepper, preferably freshly
ground

Crème fraîche

Sliced almonds, toasted (page 100)

¼ cup extra-virgin olive oil plus
more for drizzling

My book group is fertile ground for great eating. Whoever is hosting the event always prepares something delicious, including this super cooling soup, the creation of Wolfie's kindergarten teacher, Julie. Don't skip the crème fraîche swirl and sliced almonds—they add tang and crunch.

PEEL AND CUT 1½ cucumbers into large chunks and set the remaining unpeeled half aside. Combine in a food processor with the yogurt, sour cream, garlic, oil, mint, salt, and plenty of pepper. Pulse, scraping down the sides, until completely smooth.

Ladle into cold bowls or refrigerate until serving. Chop the remaining cucumber into fine dice and divide among the bowls. Swirl some crème fraîche into each bowl, drizzle with a bit of olive oil, and scatter with mint and almonds.

Per serving (when serving 4): *226 calories, 9 g protein, 7 g carbohydrates, 19 g total fat, 5 g saturated fat, 1 g fiber, 413 mg sodium*

Per serving (when serving 6): *150 calories, 6 g protein, 4 g carbohydrates, 13 g total fat, 3 g saturated fat, 1 g fiber, 275 mg sodium*

Cappelletti in Brodo

YIELD

Makes 250 pieces and 6 quarts of broth / Serves 16 as a generous main course

BROTH

2 whole chickens (3½ pounds each)

2 carrots

2 ribs celery

2 yellow onions

Kosher salt

PASTA FILLING

1 tablespoon vegetable oil

1–1¼ pounds boneless sirloin steak

Kosher salt and freshly ground black pepper

¼ pound boneless pork chops

½ pound boneless, skinless chicken breasts

2 eggs, lightly beaten

¼ cup (½ stick) unsalted butter, melted

¼ cup finely grated Pecorino Romano cheese

½ teaspoon nutmeg

½ teaspoon kosher salt

PASTA

4–5 cups all-purpose flour

6 eggs, lightly beaten

2 tablespoons olive oil

Freshly shaved Parmigiano-Reggiano cheese, for garnish

Making this soup takes time, dexterity, and patience, but it's worth every minute. My Aunt Adeline always makes it in big batches and freezes it. She used to hand-grind the meat, but now there are attachments for your stand mixer that will do that. Preparing homemade stock is something everyone should do at least once, but if time isn't on your side, use reduced-sodium chicken broth instead.

TO MAKE THE BROTH: Place the chickens, carrots, celery, and onions in a large soup pot and cover with water by 2" (8 to 10 quarts). Bring to a boil slowly. Once the broth has come to a boil, reduce the heat and bring it to a simmer. Skim the foam from the surface of the liquid with a spoon. Simmer 1½ hours. Season to taste with salt. Strain the broth through a fine-mesh sieve or a strainer lined with a dampened piece of cheesecloth folded several times. The broth can be refrigerated in a container with a tight-fitting lid for up to 1 week or frozen for up to 6 months.

TO MAKE THE PASTA FILLING: Heat the oil in a medium sauté pan (not nonstick) over medium-high heat until shimmering. Season the steak all over with salt and pepper, then sauté until nicely browned on both sides and cooked to medium, 10 minutes total. Transfer the steak to a plate. Season the pork all over with salt and pepper, and sauté until well browned on both sides and cooked through, about 10 minutes total. Transfer the pork to the plate with the steak. Season the chicken all over with salt and pepper and cook until well browned on one side, about 5 minutes. Turn the chicken, add ¼ cup water to the pan, cover, and simmer until cooked through, about 10 minutes more. Transfer the chicken to the plate with the other meats. Let cool slightly.

Cut the meats into 2" chunks. Whisk together the eggs and butter. Working in batches, place the meat in a blender or food processor. Pulse the meat, moistening with eggs and butter as necessary. Add the cheese, nutmeg, and ¼ teaspoon of the salt and pulse together until the meat has the consistency of tuna fish salad. Cover with plastic wrap and refrigerate.

TO MAKE THE PASTA: Mound 3 cups of the flour on a large wooden cutting board and make a well in the middle, going all the way through to the board. Keep 1 more cup of flour nearby, and use it to flour your board and dough if either become sticky. Pour the eggs into the well and use a fork to beat the flour into the egg, going around the perimeter of the well to prevent the walls of the well from breaking. (Have a large flat spatula or a bench scraper ready, so that if a leak does break through, you can quickly scrape some flour into it.) Continue mixing together with a fork until it begins to come together as dough, then switch to mixing by hand. Add additional flour if the ball is too sticky, or a few drops of water if it gets too dry. Knead the dough until it becomes smooth and slightly sticky to the touch, about 10 minutes.

Cut the dough into several small pieces and lightly oil each piece. Place all but one of the pieces in a bowl and cover with plastic wrap.

You can shape the pasta one of two ways: by hand, with a rolling pin, or using a pasta machine. To use the rolling pin method, lightly dust a clean wooden cutting board and rolling pin with flour. Roll out a piece of dough lightly from the center. When it begins to flatten out, start rolling from the edge of the pasta closest to you, and roll the dough up onto the rolling pin. Flour the dough well. Continue rolling and moving your hands from the center of the dough outward to the edges to thin it. Unroll and re-flour as necessary, until the dough is as thin as a dime.

To use the pasta machine method, feed a piece of dough through the widest setting of the machine, then fold over and feed it through again two more times, dusting generously with flour each time. Narrow the rollers by two notches and feed the dough through. Narrow the rollers two notches more and feed the dough through. Narrow the rollers to the thinnest setting and feed it through.

Cut into $1\frac{1}{2}$" squares. Line several large baking sheets with clean towels. Working quickly, dab about $\frac{1}{4}$ teaspoon of filling into the center of a pasta square and fold the dough shut into a triangle, pressing the edges together well. Place your pointer finger (pointing at yourself) against the fold, and wrap the two outer corners of the dough around your finger, pinching it tightly shut. If the dough

(continued)

Pasta, with Love

WHEN I WAS LITTLE, my whole family would get together at my Aunt Adeline's for holiday dinners. One Christmas, on the way to her house, my father's car got stuck in a snowstorm. I got out and walked the rest of the way. My aunt served Cappelletti in Brodo, my favorite. Coming in from the cold, I had never tasted anything as good. Ever since then, I have tried to duplicate what I ate that night. But up until a few years ago, I never got the pasta quite right. Then I visited my aunt, and she had bagfuls of it in her freezer. It was like seeing the gold in Fort Knox. I complained that I couldn't get mine like hers. She said to quit worrying, that mine was perfect the way I made it. I understood, and I spent the next few years perfecting my recipe, which is what you have here. The trick is to turn the dough with confidence and serve it to people you love.

becomes difficult to seal, moisten with a little water. Remove the pasta from your finger and place on the towel. Repeat with the remaining dough and filling. Do not let the pasta pieces touch each other.

Bring the broth to a boil and drop in the cappelletti. Return to a boil, then reduce to a simmer and set the timer for 8 minutes. Serve hot in shallow bowls with a little Parmesan sprinkled on top.

Per serving: *436 calories, 41 g protein, 27 g carbohydrates, 17 g total fat, 5 g saturated fat, 1 g fiber, 615 mg sodium*

GAZPACHO

Tom *loooooves* tomatoes, which is why they appear so often in this book. Apart from eating them sliced and drizzled with balsamic vinegar, he loves them chopped in this classic soup. We like it on the chunkier side, so we only blend half, but feel free to blend it all for an entirely smooth base. I tend to change up the proportions of the vinegar and lemon juice based on tasting the mixture as I go, and I encourage you to do the same. Don't make the mistake I once did by putting all of the cilantro into the blender—it turns the soup an unappetizing green.

COMBINE THE TOMATOES, scallions, bell pepper, garlic, tomato juice, oil, tomato paste, vinegar, lemon juice, lime juice, salt, and cayenne in a large glass or stainless steel bowl. Stir to combine. Cover and refrigerate overnight.

Transfer half of the mixture to a blender, add 2 teaspoons of the cilantro, and puree to the desired consistency. Pour back into the bowl. Refrigerate until serving time, if desired. Stir once, garnish with the avocado and cilantro leaves, and serve cold.

Per serving (when serving 6): *186 calories, 3 g protein, 15 g carbohydrates, 15 g total fat, 2 g saturated fat, 5 g fiber, 716 mg sodium*

Per serving (when serving 8): *139 calories, 2 g protein, 11 g carbohydrates, 11 g total fat, 2 g saturated fat, 4 g fiber, 537 mg sodium*

YIELD
Serves 6–8

8 fresh plum or heirloom tomatoes, majority of the seeds discarded, or 6 canned San Marzano tomatoes, drained, juices reserved and roughly chopped

10 scallions, finely chopped

1 small yellow bell pepper, cored, seeded, and roughly chopped

2 cloves garlic, pushed through a press

2 cans (5.5 ounces each) low-sodium tomato juice

¼ cup tomato paste

¼ cup good-quality extra-virgin olive oil

2 tablespoons sherry vinegar

2 tablespoons freshly squeezed lemon juice

2 tablespoons freshly squeezed lime juice

1½ teaspoons kosher salt

¼ teaspoon cayenne, or more to taste

1 avocado, sliced in wedges for garnish

Leaves from ½ bunch fresh cilantro for garnish

Grilled Chicken Vegetable Soup

There are some recipes that come from outside of my family and friends that I simply never forget. This is one of them. It's inspired by a soup I had at the Golden Door spa 25 years ago, before I had Wolfie. It's a beautiful, clean, light soup—a spa soup, if you will. The method may seem fussy, but preparing the broth, vegetables, and barley individually results in a crystal-clear broth.

COAT A GRILL rack with oil and preheat the grill on high for 5 minutes. Rub a little oil all over the chicken breast and season all over with salt and pepper. Reduce the heat to medium-high and grill the chicken, over direct heat, with the cover closed, until cooked through, turning once, about 12 minutes. (If the chicken is not cooked after 12 minutes, but is significantly browned on both sides, move it to an indirect heat spot on the grill and continue to cook.) Set aside and keep warm.

Bring the broth and bay leaf to a simmer in a medium saucepan, then turn off the heat, cover, and set aside.

Bring a few inches of water to a boil in a small saucepan and salt the water. Add the carrot, celery, and zucchini and return to a boil. Cook until just tender, for about 2 minutes. Drain and rinse with cold water. Fill the same small saucepan with ½ cup fresh water, bring to a boil, add salt, and cook the barley according to package instructions, until tender. Drain and rinse.

Place the chicken breast on a cutting board and slice crosswise into thin slices. Reheat the broth if necessary. Discard the bay leaf.

Spoon the vegetables and barley into serving bowls, then add the hot broth. Lay several slices of chicken over the surface of each bowl.

Per serving: *113 calories, 14 g protein, 8 g carbohydrates, 2 g total fat, 0.5 g saturated fat, 2 g fiber, 460 mg sodium*

YIELD

Serves 6

Extra-virgin olive oil

12 to 14-ounces boneless, skinless chicken breast

Kosher salt and freshly ground black pepper

4 cups reduced-sodium chicken broth

1 bay leaf

1 carrot, finely chopped

1 rib celery, finely chopped

1 small zucchini, finely chopped (use pieces with skin only)

¼ cup pearl barley

RIBOLLITA

YIELD

Serves 6

1 onion, chopped

1 carrot, chopped

1 rib celery, preferably with leaves, chopped

Kosher salt

1 tablespoon extra-virgin olive oil plus additional for drizzling

1 can (28 ounces) whole tomatoes, cut up

3 cups reduced-sodium vegetable broth

¼ teaspoon dried thyme or 1 sprig fresh

Freshly ground black pepper

1 bunch Tuscan kale, center stems removed and discarded, leaves coarsely chopped

1 can (10 ounces) cannellini beans, rinsed and drained

2 large slices peasant bread, cut into chunks

Freshly shaved Parmigiano-Reggiano cheese

Talk about comfort food. I will never forget Pierluigi, the vintner at Tenuta Torciano in San Gimignano (the same little town where Tom and I ate Lasagna alla Besciamella, page 135), where we tasted wine after wine and Tom had his life-changing ribollita. Essentially a peasant soup, it is a combination of beans, vegetables, and leftover bread. If it doesn't sound that appetizing, I beg you to make it and find out for yourself just how satisfying it is.

SAUTÉ THE ONION, carrot, celery, and a pinch of salt in the oil in a large Dutch oven or soup pot, over low heat, covered, stirring occasionally, until soft, about 7 minutes. Add the tomatoes (with juice), broth, and thyme and bring to a boil. Reduce to a simmer and cook, partially covered, until the vegetables begin to become tender, about 15 minutes. Season with salt and pepper.

Add the kale and simmer, covered, until the kale is soft, about 15 minutes. Add the beans and bread and simmer on low until the bread starts to soften, about 5 minutes. Serve bowls of soup with drizzles of oil and cheese.

Per serving: *232 calories, 10 g protein, 25 g carbohydrates, 11 g total fat, 2.5 g saturated fat, 5 g fiber, 520 mg sodium*

No-Knead Bertinelli Bread

My aunts and my mom made most everything from scratch, including their bread. The only thing my Aunt Adeline consumed out of a box was wine—and we used to tease her relentlessly about it! I have long tried to replicate her bread with so-so results. I gave it another go with the no-knead method. This is true to the women in my family in spirit, texture, and flavor, but is much better suited to a busy life.

YIELD
Makes 1 (10") loaf / Serves 8–10

1½ cups bread flour

1½ cups white whole wheat flour

1¾ teaspoons kosher salt

½ teaspoon active dry yeast

1½ tablespoons honey

Wheat bran for dusting

WHISK TOGETHER THE flours, salt, and yeast in a large bowl. Add the honey and 1½ cups water at room temperature and stir until the dough is uniform. Cover the bowl and set in a warm spot to rise until the dough at least triples in size, 12 to 24 hours.

Dust a work surface generously with flour, and scrape the dough out of the bowl with a spoon or rounded bench scraper and onto the work surface. Fold the dough in thirds, like a letter. Dust a clean kitchen towel generously with wheat bran, and place the dough on top, seam side down. Sprinkle the top with more wheat bran, and fold the towel over the top or cover with a second towel. Let rise until doubled in size, 1½ to 2 hours.

Meanwhile, 45 minutes before baking, place a Dutch oven or cast-iron pot with a tight-fitting lid on the bottom rack of the oven, and preheat to 475°F.

When the dough is ready, remove the preheated pot from the oven, uncover it, and flip the dough into it so that it lands seam side up. Cover the pot and place back in the oven to bake for 30 minutes.

Remove the lid and continue baking until very dark brown all over, 15 minutes more. With oven mitts, transfer the loaf to a cooling rack and allow to cool completely before slicing.

Per serving (when serving 8): *196 calories, 6 g protein, 40 g carbohydrates, 1 g total fat, 0 g saturated fat, 4 g fiber, 509 mg sodium*

Per serving (when serving 10): *160 calories, 5 g protein, 32 g carbohydrates, 0.5 g total fat, 0 g saturated fat, 3 g fiber, 408 mg sodium*

THE WORLD'S EASIEST QUICKBREAD

YIELD

Makes 1 loaf / Serves 8

3 cups self-rising flour

3 tablespoons sugar

1 can or bottle (12 ounces) warm beer

Whip this together and get it into the oven before you begin preparing the rest of dinner, and it will be ready—and still warm—by the time everyone sits down.

PREHEAT THE OVEN to 375°F. Line a 8½" x 4½" x 2½" loaf pan with parchment paper so that it overhangs on the long sides.

Whisk together the flour, sugar, and beer in a large bowl until evenly incorporated, yet slightly lumpy. Transfer to the prepared loaf pan. Bake until golden and a skewer inserted into the center comes out clean, 50 to 55 minutes. Grasp the parchment overhang and pull the loaf out of the pan and cool on a rack. Cut into 1" slices and serve.

Per serving: *204 calories, 5 g protein, 41 g carbohydrates, 0 g total fat, 0 g saturated fat, 1 g fiber, 600 mg sodium*

FRENCH-STYLE TUNA MELTS

I *lived* on tuna melts with Muenster when I first moved away from home. It was the easiest lunch and/or dinner for me to make back then—in my toaster oven. The funny thing is, Muenster doesn't hold much appeal anymore. Now I go for Gruyère and a hard-boiled egg in my melt, which takes it from a diner staple to something a bit more, well, chic?

PUT THE TUNA in a medium bowl. Add the onion, capers, olives, lemon juice, parsley, and mayonnaise and mix until thoroughly incorporated. Season to taste with pepper.

Preheat the broiler. Place the bread slices on a broiler pan and divide the tuna salad between them. Divide the egg slices between them and top each with 2 tomato slices followed by the cheese. Broil until the cheese is melted, 1 to 2 minutes. Season to taste with additional pepper.

Per serving: *399 calories, 33 g protein, 16 g carbohydrates, 22 g total fat, 8 g saturated fat, 2 g fiber, 816 mg sodium*

YIELD
Serves 2

1 can (5.5 ounces) good-quality Italian tuna packed in water, drained

¼ onion, finely chopped

1 tablespoon capers, rinsed

3 Niçoise olives, pitted and chopped

Juice of ½ lemon

¼ cup loosely packed fresh flat-leaf parsley leaves, chopped

1 tablespoon mayonnaise

Freshly ground black pepper

2 large slices good-quality bread, lightly toasted

1 hard-boiled egg, sliced (see page 51)

½ tomato, cut in 4 thin slices

½ cup grated Gruyère cheese

MOM'S PERFECT SUB SANDWICH

YIELD

Makes 4

2 tablespoons extra-virgin olive oil

2 teaspoons red wine vinegar

¼ teaspoon dried oregano

Pinch kosher salt and freshly ground black pepper

2 (6") ciabbatta rolls

¼ pound thinly sliced prosciutto

¼ pound thinly sliced capicola (preferably hot)

2 ounces thinly sliced Genoa salami

¼ pound thinly sliced provolone cheese

1 plum tomato, very thinly sliced

¾ cup shredded lettuce

¼ onion, very thinly sliced

4 pickled pepperoncini, thinly sliced

Basil, cut into thin strips (optional)

When I was pregnant with Wolfie, I craved these. Craved them. Along with Japanese pears (good thing!), I'm not sure I ate much else. The key to the perfect sub, to my mind, is the dressing, a simple mixture of olive oil, red wine vinegar, and dried oregano. My mother always sprinkled the dressing ingredients on individually, but I whisk them together so that I can taste it as I go. These make excellent picnic sandwiches—they taste even better about an hour after they're made. Wrap them tightly in foil to let the flavors meld.

STIR TOGETHER THE oil, vinegar, oregano, and salt and pepper to taste.

Using a serrated knife, slice open the rolls. Drizzle half the dressing on the roll bottoms. Divide the cold cuts, cheese, and toppings evenly among the bottom rolls. Top with the basil, if using. Drizzle the remaining dressing on the top halves of the rolls and place on top of the cold cuts to make sandwiches. Slice in half and serve.

Per serving: *308 calories, 16 g protein, 19 g carbohydrates, 18 g total fat, 6 g saturated fat, 1 g fiber, 1,239 mg sodium*

QUICK FLATBREAD PIZZA GRAZIELLA

I met Graziella in a restaurant in Malibu in the most casual way: She was speaking Italian, and my ears perked up. We bonded over our passion for food and became fast friends. When she first came to my house, we cooked together, naturally, and came up with these crispy pizzas. While the flatbreads bake, toss the greens—but resist putting them on top until just before serving. If you're feeling indulgent, top the flatbreads with thinly sliced artisanal *salumi* or pitted olives before putting them in the oven.

YIELD
Serves 4

4 flour tortillas (8" diameter)

1 teaspoon extra-virgin olive oil plus additional for brushing tortillas

½ recipe Perfect Pesto (below)

4 ounces fresh mozzarella, very thinly sliced

1 cup cherry tomatoes, halved

4 cups baby arugula

1 tablespoon freshly squeezed lemon juice

PREHEAT THE OVEN to 375°F. Place the tortillas on a large baking sheet. Brush each with some oil, then toast in the oven until golden, about 3 minutes. Spread 2 tablespoons of the pesto on each tortilla. Divide the mozzarella equally among the tortillas and arrange on top, followed by the tomatoes. Return the tortillas to the oven and bake until the cheese is melted, about 7 minutes.

MEANWHILE, PUT THE arugula in a serving bowl and add the 1 teaspoon oil and the lemon juice, adding more lemon juice to taste, if desired. Toss to thoroughly coat. Divide the greens evenly among the baked tortillas, piling them in the center of each. Serve immediately.

PERFECT PESTO

YIELD
Makes about 1 cup

COMBINE THE BASIL, garlic, pine nuts, Parmigiano-Reggiano, Pecorino Romano, salt, and pepper in a food processor or blender. Pulse until all of the ingredients are finely chopped. With the motor running, add the oil in a steady stream. Taste and adjust seasoning.

Per serving: *349 calories, 14 g protein, 34 g carbohydrates, 20 g total fat, 6 g saturated fat, 12 g fiber, 530 mg sodium*

5 cups loosely packed fresh basil leaves

3 cloves garlic, sliced

¼ cup pine nuts

¼ cup finely grated Parmigiano-Reggiano cheese

¼ cup finely grated Pecorino Romano cheese

½ teaspoon kosher salt

Freshly ground black pepper

¼ cup extra-virgin olive oil

Salads

They get you to connect with
ingredients in their purest form.

S ALADS ARE AMONG the most maligned and mismanaged of meals. Too many people frequently ruin a good thing with calorie-heavy toppings and fatty dressings. They turn a potentially amazing food experience into a minefield of regret and depression. My intent is to get you to look at salads as a way to connect to food in its purest form. It's a chance to think about texture and flavor, taste and nutrition, and even the preparation that goes into a salad long before you pull the ingredients together.

Think about it. Most of the fixings that we put into salads begin with seeds that people have planted, cultivated, picked, and shipped to markets. When I eat the lettuce, radishes, beans, vegetables, and nuts that go into my salads, I feel closer to this timeless process of planting and harvesting, and more connected to the earth. It inspires me to want to be healthy. I say this without being a crunchie-granola-hippie type, not that there's anything wrong with that. But I have reached an age where I care about what I put into my body. I'm equally concerned about what I buy and who I support. I try to buy the best-quality ingredients I can find.

Salads get straight to the point. They are the nudist colonies of meals. You see all of your ingredients as they really are, raw and undressed. It affects your perspective. If you're like me, you want fresh ingredients. You won't shop just once a week and see the food you bought on the weekend start to go bad the following Friday. I did that for years. Now I stop by the store on my way home from work. On weekends, I make a trip to the local farmers' market. I used to tell people it was worth the effort, but then I realized it's not an effort. In fact, I look forward to visiting the farmers. Plus I find that organic produce holds up longer than its nonorganic counterparts, and I'm not throwing out food at the end of the week.

The salads in this chapter were chosen for a variety of reasons, ranging from the simple nostalgia I have for Mom's Thanksgiving Salad (page 108) to the wonderful times I've had making Angela's Roasted Corn and Bean Salad (page 110), which we traditionally put on the menu at family get-togethers and enlist lots of helpers so we can catch up as we chop ingredients at the counter. Tom's What's-on-Hand Salad (page 119) is just practical—and good, for your health and your pocketbook! Basically, he uses every fresh vegetable in the house before it goes bad. Smart, right?

I have a simple rule when it comes to salads. I build them around ingredients I love. Tom is a fan of beets. I like fennel. I use three basic cheeses: Roquefort, feta, and goat. I usually mix nuts in, too—mainly pine nuts, walnuts, or hazelnuts.

Like I did, you'll discover that these salads can serve as a starter, lunch, or even dinner, when they're a combination of vegetables with chicken or shrimp tossed on top. Beyond their versatility, though, my favorite part is that salads vary according to the season. Caprese salads are best during tomato season, and I think the Winter Salad (page 113)—pear, walnuts, and blue cheese—is heavenly with a glass of wine and a blazing fireplace. Once you get the hang of making salads, switch things up, the way Tom and I do, depending on what's fresh and available. Once I discovered salads that worked for me, I found that I was willing to go the extra mile to find the finest ingredients and take the time to prepare them well.

CLASSIC GREEK SALAD

With California's long growing season, we seem to have the ingredients for this salad in the house for many months of the year. As with any salad that includes cheese, it can easily go from healthy to hefty, so I tend to go for reduced-fat feta cheese for this one. Tom prefers green peppers in the mix. Me? Not so much, so I add them to his after I've served myself.

COMBINE THE VINEGAR, lemon juice, oregano, and salt and pepper to taste in a small bowl and whisk together. Add the oil in a steady stream, whisking constantly.

Combine the lettuce, onion, bell pepper (if using), tomato, cucumber, olives, and feta in a large salad bowl. Pour the dressing over and toss until all of the ingredients are well coated. Taste and adjust seasonings, adding more salt or lemon juice as desired.

Per serving (when serving 2): *292 calories, 10 g protein, 11 g carbohydrates, 24 g total fat, 3 g saturated fat, 3 g fiber, 590 mg sodium*

Per serving (when serving 4): *146 calories, 5 g protein, 5 g carbohydrates, 12 g total fat, 2 g saturated fat, 1 g fiber, 295 mg sodium*

YIELD
Serves 2 for lunch or 4 as a side

1½ teaspoons red wine vinegar

1½ teaspoons freshly squeezed lemon juice

½ teaspoon dried oregano

Kosher salt and freshly ground black pepper

3 tablespoons extra-virgin olive oil

8 large leaves red leaf lettuce, sliced crosswise

¼ red onion, thinly sliced

½ green bell pepper, thinly sliced (optional)

1 vine-ripened tomato, sliced into thin wedges

1 small cucumber, peeled if waxy, sliced

6 kalamata olives

2 ounces fat-free feta cheese, crumbled

GREENS WITH POLENTA CROUTONS

YIELD

Serves 6 as a side salad

½ recipe Polenta (below), cooled and firmed

1 teaspoon Dijon mustard

2 tablespoons balsamic vinegar

¼ cup extra-virgin olive oil

10 cups (5 ounces) mixed baby greens

½ cup cherry tomatoes, halved

2 tablespoons dried cranberries or currants

⅓ cup crumbled Roquefort cheese

Kosher salt and freshly ground black pepper

I am constantly trying to reproduce at home the dishes I eat in restaurants. This one, a favorite on the menu at Sparks, an American grill not far from my house, could not be easier. I prefer homemade polenta, but if you're pressed for time, you can use the prepared polenta that comes in a tube.

PREHEAT THE OVEN to 400°F. Line a baking sheet with parchment paper or nonstick silicone liner. Unmold the polenta and cut into 12 to 16 equal rectangles. Bake until crisp and golden, about 1 hour.

Meanwhile, whisk together the mustard and vinegar in a small bowl. Add the oil in a thin stream, whisking constantly.

Toss the greens with the dressing in a large salad bowl. Add the tomatoes, cranberries, and cheese, and toss again. Season to taste with salt and pepper. Divide the salad equally among 6 plates and arrange 2 croutons on top of each. Serve immediately.

POLENTA

YIELD

Makes about 3 cups

2 teaspoons kosher salt

1 cup instant polenta

1 tablespoon unsalted butter

½ cup grated cheese, such as Parmigiano-Reggiano, Pecorino Romano, fontina, or Gruyère

1 tablespoon chopped fresh oregano or rosemary leaves

COAT AN 8" x 8" baking dish with a thin coat of olive oil.

Combine 4 cups water and the salt in a medium saucepan and bring to a boil over high heat. Slowly add the polenta, whisking constantly. Reduce the heat to low, bringing the polenta to a simmer, and cook, stirring occasionally, until thick, about 15 minutes. Turn off the heat and stir in the butter, cheese, and herbs. Serve warm immediately. Or cool to make croutons by pouring the polenta into the prepared dish and cool completely until firm.

Per serving: *187 calories, 5 g protein, 17 g carbohydrates, 12 g total fat, 4 g saturated fat, 3 g fiber, 498 mg sodium*

BUTTER LETTUCE SALAD

Osteria Mozza, Nancy Silverton's acclaimed LA restaurant with Mario Batali and Joe Bastianich, has not only tortellini in brodo (see page 72 for my Nonnie's version!) on the menu but also this salad, which is to die for. For some reason, it wasn't on the menu the last time I was there, and it turns out that the staff had seen my reservation and were not happy to have to tell me that. I guess I left an impression! I'm no Nancy Silverton, but I love the version I make at home—my homage to Mozza.

WHISK TO COMBINE the vinegar, oil, chives, and salt and pepper to taste in a bowl. Toss the lettuce with the dressing in a large salad bowl. Divide the lettuce between two large bowls or plates. Divide the pancetta, eggs, nuts, and cheese between the two, layering them in that order.

Per serving (when serving 2): *475 calories, 16 g protein, 5 g carbohydrates, 45 g total fat, 11 g saturated fat, 1 g fiber, 747 mg sodium*

Per serving (when serving 4): *237 calories, 8 g protein, 2 g carbohydrates, 23 g total fat, 5 g saturated fat, 1 g fiber, 374 mg sodium*

YIELD

Serves 2 for lunch or 4 as a side

1 tablespoon white balsamic vinegar

3 tablespoons extra-virgin olive oil

1 tablespoon chopped fresh chives

Kosher salt and freshly ground black pepper

1 head butter lettuce, separated into leaves

2 thin slices pancetta or bacon, cooked until crisp and broken into bite-size pieces

2 hard-boiled eggs (see page 51), halved and lightly salted and peppered

¼ cup toasted hazelnuts, roughly chopped

1½ ounces Roquefort cheese, crumbled

HELEN'S ORANGE SALAD

YIELD

Serves 4

1 teaspoon Dijon mustard

1 tablespoon white balsamic vinegar

¼ cup extra-virgin olive oil

3 cups baby arugula

2 navel oranges

1 blood orange

1 bulb fennel, thinly sliced

¼ red onion (or more), sliced into thin rings

8 leaves fresh basil, cut into thin strips

Kosher coarse salt and freshly ground black pepper

This is a version of my mother-in-law's amazing salad, one that she only makes in January and February when the blood oranges are ripe. I love fennel in anything, so I added thin slices of it because the combination of sweet oranges and anise is addictive. Make sure to slice the fennel thinly—I sometimes use a mandoline, but a very sharp chef's knife will do the trick.

WHISK TOGETHER THE mustard and vinegar in a small bowl. Slowly add the oil in a thin stream, whisking constantly until fully emulsified. If the dressing breaks while you're making it—believe me, it happens to me!—stop pouring the oil and whisk what you've made so far until it comes together again.

Spread the arugula on a large platter. Slice off the top and bottom of each orange. Cut away the peel and outer membranes, then separate the orange into segments. Using a paring knife, cut away the membranes from each segment. Layer the orange slices over the arugula, followed by the fennel, onion (add more to taste), and basil. Season with salt and pepper. Pour the vinaigrette on top, toss, and serve immediately.

Per serving: *200 calories, 2 g protein, 19 g carbohydrates, 14 g total fat, 2 g saturated fat, 4 g fiber, 65 mg sodium*

TOM'S SUMMER SALAD

I tease Tom that he'll call anything a dish if it's a good vehicle for tomatoes. This is one of those salads that wholly depends on the quality of the ingredients—there's no faking it. The tomatoes should never have seen the inside of a refrigerator, and the cucumbers should be garden fresh. This is an excellent side dish to serve with Tom's other brilliant dish, Chicken Paillard with Salsa Verde (page 138).

(page 138)

YIELD

Serves 4–6

1 tablespoon balsamic vinegar

¼ cup extra-virgin olive oil

Kosher salt and freshly ground black pepper

Sugar (optional)

2 cucumbers, peeled and halved lengthwise, then thickly sliced

Several thick slices of red onion, halved if large, separated into rings

3 large tomatoes, thickly sliced and halved

WHISK TOGETHER THE vinegar, oil, salt, and pepper in a small bowl. Taste and add sugar, if desired.

Combine the cucumbers, onion, and tomatoes in a large bowl and toss to combine. Pour the vinaigrette over and toss again to thoroughly coat. Season with salt and pepper to taste. Let sit at room temperature, tossing occasionally, for about 30 minutes before serving.

Per serving (when serving 4): *170 calories, 2 g protein, 10 g carbohydrates, 14 g total fat, 2 g saturated fat, 3 g fiber, 70 mg sodium*

Per serving (when serving 6): *110 calories, 1 g protein, 7 g carbohydrates, 10 g total fat, 1.5 g saturated fat, 2 g fiber, 47 mg sodium*

BEET, ONION, AND FETA SALAD

YIELD
Serves 4

2 large beets, red, orange, and/or gold, trimmed and scrubbed

Grated zest of 1 lime (about 1 teaspoon)

Juice of 1 lime (about 2 tablespoons)

2 tablespoons canola oil

1 teaspoon honey

½ red onion, sliced into thin rings

Freshly ground black pepper

2 ounces feta cheese, crumbled

2 tablespoons toasted crushed hazelnuts (see note)

I used to bypass the beets at the farmers' market because I never felt confident about cooking them. But honestly, there's nothing more to it than roasting and peeling. Now, if you don't want your hands to stain, you can protect them by putting a bunched-up paper towel in each hand before handling them or by wearing latex gloves. These days, specialty food stores carry excellent packaged cooked beets—use them if time is tight.

PREHEAT THE OVEN to 400°F. Place the beets in a small roasting dish, covered tightly with foil, and bake until easily pierced all the way through with a paring knife, about 1 hour and 15 minutes, depending on the size of the beets. Let them cool for about 10 minutes.

Meanwhile, whisk together the lime zest and juice, oil, and honey in a small bowl.

Use a bunched-up paper towel in each hand to rub off the beet skins (use a vegetable peeler for any stubborn bits). Slice the beets into thin wedges and place in a salad bowl. Put the onions over the top and pour the dressing over. Toss to thoroughly coat and season with pepper. Sprinkle the feta and hazelnuts over the salad and serve warm.

Per serving: *150 calories, 3 g protein, 8 g carbohydrates, 12 g total fat, 3 g saturated fat, 2 g fiber, 190 mg sodium*

HOW TO TOAST NUTS

Toasting nuts makes them taste more, well, nutty. To toast them on the stove top, put them in a dry skillet over medium heat and cook, stirring, until golden and fragrant. To toast them in the oven, spread in a single layer on a baking sheet and roast at 350°F until golden and fragrant.

CAPRESE SALAD

YIELD
Serves 4

1 ball (7 ounces) fresh buffalo mozzarella, packed in water, thinly sliced

2 vine-ripened tomatoes, thinly sliced

Extra-virgin olive oil

Kosher coarse salt and freshly ground black pepper

Fresh basil or mint leaves, sliced into thick ribbons

Vincotto

We recently started growing heirloom tomatoes in the backyard. I have Cydney, a *Hot in Cleveland* colleague, to thank for the seedlings. Wish me luck! Tomato season is the only time to prepare this classic Italian antipasto, and it should only be made with fresh mozzarella packed in water. Don't be tempted to buy the kind in the plastic package from the supermarket: You'll never know the real beauty of a caprese. Gourmet or good Italian markets are your best bets. While you're there, pick up a bottle of vincotto, which literally translated is "cooked wine," and is wonderful for drizzling—on this and on roasted vegetables.

ARRANGE THE MOZZARELLA and tomato slices on a platter, alternating and overlapping them. Drizzle generously with oil, then sprinkle with salt and pepper. Scatter basil on top. Drizzle with vincotto. Let it sit for 5 minutes and serve.

Per serving: *243 calories, 11 g protein, 4 g carbohydrates, 21 g total fat, 9 g saturated fat, 1 g fiber, 169 mg sodium*

Chicken Salad with Apples and Grapes

Yes, there *is* a way to make chicken salad without gobs of mayonnaise. There's just 1 tablespoon of the real thing here, which, along with low-fat plain yogurt and low-fat buttermilk, is all you need to give it very full body. This is one of my favorite lunches to pack on workdays. It's completely satisfying, with just the right combination of smoky chicken, crisp tart apple, tangy vinegar, and creamy dressing.

COMBINE THE YOGURT, buttermilk, mayonnaise, vinegar, curry, garlic, salt, and pepper in a medium bowl and whisk to incorporate. Combine the chicken, apple, grapes, and watercress in a large salad bowl. Pour the dressing over and toss to thoroughly coat. Taste and adjust the salt, pepper, and curry powder as desired. Arrange a lettuce leaf on each of 4 salad plates. Divide the salad evenly among the plates and serve.

Per serving: *190 calories, 21 g protein, 12 g carbohydrates, 6 g total fat, 1.5 g saturated fat, 1 g fiber, 328 mg sodium*

YIELD
Serves 4

¼ cup low-fat plain yogurt

¼ cup low-fat buttermilk

1 tablespoon mayonnaise

2 tablespoons cider vinegar

1 teaspoon curry powder

1 clove garlic, pushed through a press

½ teaspoon kosher salt

Copious amounts of freshly ground black pepper

2 cups roughly chopped grilled chicken

½ Granny Smith apple, skin on, cored and chopped into large cubes

¾ cup red grapes, halved

1 cup loosely packed watercress or fresh flat-leaf parsley, chopped

4 large romaine lettuce leaves

Japanese Marinated Cucumber Salad

YIELD
Serves 4

Sunomono is on the menu at pretty much every Japanese restaurant. And it's always my first course. It could not be healthier and is so delicious. It's a great salad to take to work because the longer it sits, the better it tastes. It makes a great side to a steak or salmon, cold or grilled.

½ cup plus 2 tablespoons unseasoned rice vinegar

2 tablespoons less sodium soy sauce

4 teaspoons sugar

4 teaspoons sesame oil

6 small cucumbers, thinly sliced on a mandoline

COMBINE THE VINEGAR, soy sauce, sugar, oil, and 1 tablespoon water in a medium bowl and whisk to combine. Add the cucumbers, cover, and let marinate in the refrigerator for at least 1 hour. Serve chilled.

Per serving: *89 calories, 2 g protein, 10 g carbohydrates, 5 g total fat, 0.5 g saturated fat, 2 g fiber, 273 mg sodium*

Fennel Salad with Goat Cheese and Pine Nuts

YIELD

Serves 2 for lunch or 4 as a side

1 tablespoon red wine vinegar

3 tablespoons extra-virgin olive oil

Kosher salt and freshly ground black pepper

3 cups loosely packed baby arugula leaves

1 bulb fennel, fronds removed and chopped, and the fennel cored and thinly sliced using a mandoline

2 ounces goat cheese, crumbled

2 tablespoons toasted pine nuts

One of the most compelling reasons to live in California just might be the wild fennel that grows near my house. I love, love fennel every which way—roasted, braised, grilled, pureed, and raw—and also love how it can go from forceful and crisp to creamy and mellow, depending on how it's prepared. This salad features very thinly sliced fennel and peppery arugula, two vegetables with big-time personalities that play well together. The flavors are intense and intensely satisfying, which is key when you're trying to eat well.

WHISK TOGETHER THE vinegar, oil, and salt and pepper to taste in a small bowl. Combine the arugula and sliced fennel in a medium salad bowl. Pour the vinaigrette over and toss to thoroughly coat. Season to taste with salt and pepper. Scatter the fennel fronds, cheese, and pine nuts on top and serve.

Per serving: (when serving 2): *370 calories, 9 g protein, 15 g carbohydrates, 33 g total fat, 9 g saturated fat, 8 g fiber, 360 mg sodium*

Per serving (when serving 4): *190 calories, 4 g protein, 7 g carbohydrates, 16 g total fat, 4.5 g saturated fat, 4 g fiber, 180 mg sodium*

Mom's Thanksgiving Salad

YIELD

Serves 8–12

¾ cup low-fat buttermilk

4 tablespoons plus 2 teaspoons low-fat mayonnaise

3 tablespoons chopped fresh chives

1 tablespoon plus 2 teaspoons cider vinegar

Juice of ¾ lemon

1 tablespoon sugar

½ teaspoon kosher salt

½ teaspoon freshly ground black pepper

8 ribs celery, sliced about ¼" thick on the diagonal

2 Gala apples, skin on, cored and diced

1 cup toasted walnuts (page 100), roughly chopped

To this day, my mother prepares this for Thanksgiving—and sometimes Christmas—along with oyster and cornbread stuffing and a molded cranberry salad. And thank God, because I never ate the stuffing and still haven't come around to liking it!

WHISK TOGETHER THE buttermilk, mayonnaise, chives, vinegar, lemon juice, sugar, salt, and pepper in a small bowl. Combine the celery, apples, and walnuts in a large bowl. Pour three-quarters of the dressing over and toss to coat. Let stand for 5 minutes at room temperature and toss again. Taste and adjust the salt. Add the remaining dressing, if desired, and toss again. Serve at room temperature.

Per serving (when serving 8): *167 calories, 4 g protein, 15 g carbohydrates, 12 g total fat, 1.5 g saturated fat, 3 g fiber, 235 mg sodium*

Per serving (when serving 12): *110 calories, 2 g protein, 10 g carbohydrates, 8 g total fat, 1 g saturated fat, 2 g fiber, 157 mg sodium*

Giving Thanks

I GREW UP THINKING that my mom's Thanksgiving salad was something that could only be made during the holidays. No one ever said that explicitly, but it was implied in the same way that stuffing and pumpkin pie seemed also to be annual events. As I grew up, though, I came to understand three things about this salad. One, it was a variation of a traditional Waldorf salad. Two, it was tied to the seasonality of apples. And three, this salad tasted even better the day after it was first served, and the day after that. It was like the rest of any holiday meal—more delicious over the weekend and even better if I was pinching a taste with my fingers. Don't ask me why. Nowadays, I substitute low-fat mayonnaise for the high-fat mayonnaise and make this throughout the fall, as long as the apples are ripe, and whenever I need a taste of healthy holiday comfort food.

Christmas, 1971, at my childhood home

ANGELA'S ROASTED CORN AND BEAN SALAD

YIELD

Serves 12–14

SALAD

4 fresh or frozen ears of corn, husk removed

1 can (15 ounces) black beans, rinsed and drained

1 can (15 ounces) kidney beans, rinsed and drained

1 can (15 ounces) chickpeas, rinsed and drained

1 green bell pepper, chopped

1 red bell pepper, chopped

½ red onion, chopped

½ jalapeño or serrano chile pepper, seeded and finely chopped (wear plastic gloves when handling)

½ cup loosely packed fresh cilantro leaves, chopped

1 teaspoon kosher salt

Freshly ground black pepper

Angela is Tom's only sister and one of the sweetest women you'd ever want to meet. When we can't see her in Ohio, she makes the trek out to California to stay with us, and I must say, when she visits, it's like we were never apart. We always end up cooking up something, and this was a favorite the last time she was out. It's definitely one of those "don't let the long ingredient list scare you" recipes, because it couldn't be easier to throw together. Even better, it serves a crowd. It's the perfect choice when there's leftover corn on the cob in the fridge.

TO MAKE THE SALAD: Preheat a grill on high for 5 minutes. Reduce the heat to medium-high and grill the corn, with the cover closed, turning occasionally, until some kernels are black, about 12 minutes. Remove and allow the corn to cool slightly.

Using a sharp knife, cut off the kernels into a very large, deep serving bowl. (Hold the narrow end of the cob, point the other end into the bowl, and cut downward, so that flying kernels are trapped by the bowl itself.) Add the beans, bell peppers, onion, chile pepper, cilantro, and salt and pepper to taste to the bowl and toss.

TO MAKE THE DRESSING: Whisk together the vinegar, lime juice, sugar, garlic, cumin, salt, chili powder, and olive oil in a small bowl. Season to taste with the hot sauce.

Pour the dressing over the salad and toss to thoroughly coat. Let sit at room temperature for 20 minutes, toss again, and serve. The salad can be made a day in advance, covered, and refrigerated. Bring to room temperature before serving.

Per serving (when serving 12): *140 calories, 5 g protein, 20 g carbohydrates, 6 g total fat, 1 g saturated fat, 4 g fiber, 452 mg sodium*

Per serving (when serving 14): *120 calories, 4 g protein, 17 g carbohydrates, 5 g total fat, 0.5 g saturated fat, 4 g fiber, 388 mg sodium*

DRESSING

1 tablespoon red wine vinegar

½ cup freshly squeezed lime juice (from about 2 large or 4 small limes)

1 tablespoon sugar

2 cloves garlic, pushed through a press

1 teaspoon ground cumin

1 teaspoon kosher salt

Pinch chili powder

¼ cup extra-virgin olive oil

Hot sauce, preferably Crystal Hot Sauce

WINTER SALAD

I was often surprised by what I could eat on the Jenny Craig diet. A salad with blue cheese and walnuts? Yep! Unlike most salads, in which you dress the greens last, this one calls for you to put the vinaigrette in the salad bowl first followed by the sliced pears, which require an acid to prevent them from browning. There are times when I add a few strips of grilled chicken to the mix and call it dinner.

WHISK TOGETHER THE mustard and vinegar in a medium bowl. Slowly add the oil in a steady stream, whisking constantly. Season with salt and pepper to taste. Halve and core the pears, then thinly slice lengthwise. Place in the vinaigrette as you go and toss to coat.

Place the lettuce in a salad bowl and season with salt and pepper. Pour the vinaigrette with the pears over and toss to evenly coat. Divide the leaves and pears among 4 salad plates. Top each with an equal amount of walnuts and cheese. Serve immediately.

Per serving: *280 calories, 4 g protein, 17 g carbohydrates, 23 g total fat, 4 g saturated fat, 4 g fiber, 220 mg sodium*

YIELD
Serves 4

1 teaspoon Dijon mustard

2 tablespoons balsamic vinegar

1/4 cup extra-virgin olive oil

Kosher salt and freshly ground black pepper

2 ripe Bosc pears

12 large leaves red romaine or red leaf lettuce, torn into bite-size pieces

1/3 cup walnuts, toasted (page 100)

1/4 cup crumbled blue cheese

Orzo with Grape Tomatoes and Radishes

ORZO SALAD

1 pound orzo

½ cup pepitas, toasted (see note below)

1½ cups grape tomatoes, halved or quartered

1 small English cucumber, peeled and diced (about 3 cups)

1 bunch radishes, sliced (about 1 cup)

1 cup kalamata olives, pitted and halved

5 ounces goat cheese or low-fat feta cheese, crumbled

2 tablespoons chopped fresh flat-leaf parsley

2 tablespoons chopped fresh mint

2 tablespoons chopped fresh basil

VINAIGRETTE

1 shallot, finely minced (about 2½ tablespoons)

1 tablespoon Dijon mustard

¼ cup freshly squeezed lemon juice (from 1 to 1½ lemons)

½ cup extra-virgin olive oil

Kosher salt and freshly ground black pepper

This is my take on one of prolific cookbook author Diane Worthington's salads. When I'm stumped for what to serve at a dinner party, I open one of her books. I've served this salad many times over the years, and started experimenting with the recipe when I found myself without some of the ingredients and didn't want to run to the store. It has proven to be quite the party pleaser.

TO MAKE THE SALAD: Bring a large pot of lightly salted water to a boil. Add the orzo and cook at a lazy boil until just tender, about 9 minutes. Transfer to a colander and drain well, then transfer to a large serving bowl. Add the pepitas, tomatoes, cucumber, radishes, olives, cheese, parsley, mint, and basil to the orzo.

TO MAKE THE VINAIGRETTE: Whisk together the shallot, mustard, and lemon juice in a small bowl. Add the oil in a steady stream whisking constantly. Season to taste with salt and pepper.

Pour the vinaigrette over the orzo salad and toss well to distribute the ingredients evenly. Serve warm or at room temperature. Or make ahead and chill.

Per serving: *548 calories, 15 g protein, 51 g carbohydrates, 33 g total fat, 7 g saturated fat, 3 g fiber, 834 mg sodium*

How to Toast Pepitas

Roasted, salted pepitas (hulled pumpkin seeds) add an excellent salty, earthy crunch to everything from salads to ice cream. To toast them, lightly coat the seeds with olive oil. Season with kosher salt, then spread in a single layer on a baking sheet. Roast at 400°F, stirring occasionally, until golden and fragrant, 5 to 8 minutes. You'll know they're almost done when you hear them start to pop.

MRS. VAN HALEN'S GADO GADO

YIELD

Serves 4

THE SALAD

- 10 ounces (about 2 cups) green beans, trimmed
- 6–8 cups broccoli or cauliflower, cut into florets
- 2½ cups carrots, cut into 3" lengths, halved lengthwise if medium in size or quartered if large
- 1 pound small new potatoes, halved or quartered if large
- 2 cucumbers, sliced into ½"-thick rounds, halved if very large
- 4 hard-boiled eggs, quartered (see page 51)
- Kosher coarse salt

This classic Indonesian salad was my introduction to vegetables tossed in a spicy peanut sauce, compliments of Ed's mother. Peanuts to Indonesians are like tomatoes to Italians—they show up in almost every dish. It's all about prep work here, but it's *so* worth it in the end. Take care not to overcook the vegetables; they should be tender but retain a slight snap. If you're using a very large steamer, check for doneness a little sooner than the times noted below.

TO MAKE THE SALAD: Place a large pot with several inches of water and fitted with a steamer basket over high heat and bring to a boil. Add the green beans, cover, and steam until bright and crisp-tender, about 10 minutes. Do not overcook. Transfer the beans to a large colander and rinse under cold water to stop the cooking. Transfer them to a large platter, keeping them in a discreet pile.

Add the broccoli to the steamer and cook until bright and crisp-tender, about 5 minutes. Transfer to the colander and rinse under cold water. Transfer to the platter.

Continue in the same fashion with the carrots and potatoes, steaming the carrots for about 7 minutes and the potatoes for 15 to 20 minutes. If serving the salad right away, do not rinse the potatoes; if preparing ahead of time, rinse them under cold water.

TO MAKE THE PEANUT SAUCE: Heat the peanut oil in a small sauté pan over medium-low heat until hot. Add the onion and chile pepper (or more to taste) and cook until softened and fragrant, about 5 minutes. Add the garlic and ginger and cook 20 seconds. Add the peanut butter, coconut milk, and chile paste, increase the heat to medium, and whisk until the mixture comes together, 2 to 3 minutes. Turn off the heat and whisk in the soy sauce, lime juice, and fish sauce. If the sauce separates before you want to serve it, whisk until it emulsifies and use immediately.

Divide the steamed vegetables, cucumbers, and eggs equally among 4 salad plates. Sprinkle salt over each. Pour the peanut sauce into small ramekins and place one in the center of each plate. Alternatively, arrange all of the vegetables and eggs on a platter and serve with the peanut sauce in a small bowl.

Per serving: *615 calories, 23 g protein, 54 g carbohydrates, 39 g total fat, 17 g saturated fat, 14 g fiber, 760 mg sodium*

PEANUT SAUCE

1½ tablespoons peanut oil

¼ cup finely chopped onion

½ jalapeño chile pepper (or more), ribs and seeds removed, finely chopped (wear plastic gloves when handling)

4 cloves garlic, pushed through a press

1½ tablespoons grated fresh ginger

½ cup creamy natural peanut butter

1 cup coconut milk (shake can well before pouring)

2 tablespoons Thai red chile paste

2 tablespoons less sodium soy sauce

6 tablespoons freshly squeezed lime juice (from 3 limes)

1 teaspoon fish sauce

THE WHAT'S-ON-HAND SALAD

Tom is not afraid to experiment in the kitchen and put together dishes without a recipe. I can't stand wasting food, perhaps a result of growing up in an Italian household where every bit was used, whether it was vegetables, bread, or pasta. We make a great pair. There's only one real instruction for this simple salad: Look in your vegetable drawer or bowl, see what you've got, and chop it all up! This recipe is inspired by *fatoosh*—the Middle Eastern salad of cucumbers, tomatoes, parsley, tart sumac, and pita pieces—when it came to the dressing here. Tangy lemon-pepper replaces signature sumac, and crushed saltines stand in for the pita. If you don't have red onion on hand, add a minced shallot or finely chopped scallions to the vinaigrette.

WHISK TOGETHER THE lemon juice and oil until emulsifies.

Combine the meat or poultry, vegetables, cheese, salad greens, onion, and herbs in a large bowl. Sprinkle with the lemon pepper. Pour the dressing over and toss to combine. Taste for seasoning (some lemon peppers are salty) and add salt and pepper to taste. Scatter the crackers across the top and toss again. Serve immediately.

Per serving: *454 calories, 31 g protein, 19 g carbohydrates, 30 g total fat, 10 g saturated fat, 5 g fiber, 402 mg sodium*

YIELD
Serves 4

2 tablespoons freshly squeezed lemon juice

¼ cup extra-virgin olive oil

2 cups cooked chopped or shredded meat or poultry, such as steak, chicken, turkey, ham, or deli meats

2 cups cooked vegetables, such as asparagus, broccoli, cauliflower, green beans, potatoes, beets, or beans

½ cup shaved hard cheese (use a vegetable peeler), such as Manchego, Parmigiano-Reggiano, Pecorino Romano, or Cheddar; or crumbled or torn soft cheese, such as blue, goat, feta, or mozzarella

10 cups salad greens, such as romaine, arugula, baby spinach, or mixed greens

2–3 tablespoons chopped red onion

½ cup fresh soft herb leaves, such as parsley, cilantro, basil, tarragon, chervil, or mint

½ teaspoon lemon pepper

Kosher salt and freshly ground black pepper

15–20 crackers, such as saltines or butter crackers, broken into bite-size pieces

Main Courses

Even the simplest meal
should be a celebration.

WHAT I LIKE about going to wonderful restaurants beyond a special meal is watching people at neighboring tables and those working in the kitchen enjoying the experience of good food. For years, I wanted that same relationship with food. I always loved to eat, but first I had to learn to love myself. Once that happened, I was able to use food to nourish my body rather than feed my emotions, and everything changed as I had hoped. I ate in moderation. I leaned back from the table when I was full, even if I hadn't finished. And most importantly, I rediscovered the taste of food, the flavors and sensuality of certain ingredients, as well as a whole new enjoyment when I sat down for a meal.

I turned into one of those people in restaurants that I had admired. I found myself appreciating what I was eating, how it had been prepared, and the effort and artistry and passion that had gone into its preparation. This led me to change my habits at the grocery store, as well. Instead of prowling the frozen food section in search of something that would fill me up, as I had done in my pre–Jenny Craig days, I spent time with the butcher inquiring about cuts of lean meat and with the fishmonger discussing the best ways to prepare certain fish and shellfish. I explored the produce section. And I arrived home blather-

ing on about cilantro and citrus as if I had discovered Mexican food for the first time.

In a way I had. My enthusiasm is now firmly planted in my kitchen. I want even the simplest meal to be a celebration. And why not? For me, it all comes together at the dinner table. These are generally life's most memorable meals. They were for me when I was growing up in Delaware, where all I wanted was to make it to the adults' table, which I never quite managed before I moved to LA.

But I've been at the big table for a while now, and the main courses I am sharing with you are dishes that I have made for years or variations of meals I have loved at restaurants or someone's home. My Mom's Spaghetti and Meatballs (page 136) is here, the same recipe she's used ever since I can remember. After I separated from Ed, I couldn't think of anything to make for dinner other than lamb chops. I varied the marinade, but one night Wolfie came home from school and said, "Don't tell me we're having lamb chops again." But I never tired of them, though—and I think you'll like the ones in the recipe that I named after him.

As in other chapters, all the main course recipes are personal. Chicken with Prunes and Olives (page 141) dates back to the first time I hosted my book club. It was my first real grown-up dinner party. Pa V's Pot Roast (page 150) was inspired by Tom's father, who made dinner for us during one of his rare visits to LA. And Mrs. Van Halen's Bami Goreng (page 146) is beyond simple and ridiculously delicious. I consider it one of Van Halen's greatest hits. And if you make Nonnie's Gnocchi (opposite page), you might as well be sitting with me looking through family photo albums. I think there's enough variety here for every taste and occasion. After you make these recipes a few times, I hope some of my favorites become yours, too.

NONNIE'S GNOCCHI

If I had a day in my childhood I could relive, it would have to be sitting in my aunt's basement watching my grandmother make gnocchi. I loved sitting at the big kitchen table with her, watching her press the dough in her palm while telling me stories of her childhood in Turin, Italy. She was always very pulled together, dressed in a good skirt and heels. For a woman who cooked as much as she did, she had a great figure. Nonnie's gnocchi are my madeleines—they take me right back to that kitchen table every time.

YIELD

Serves 6

2 pounds russet potatoes

2 cups all-purpose flour plus more for dusting surfaces

¼ teaspoon kosher salt

3 cups Meat Ragu (page 134)

PREHEAT THE OVEN to 375°F. Scrub the potatoes well and pierce in several places with the tip of a knife. Bake on a baking sheet until cooked through, about 1 hour. Set aside to cool.

Once they're cool enough to handle, peel the potatoes and pass the flesh through a ricer or the finest holes of a food mill. Place 1½ cups of the flour on a clean work surface and put the potatoes in the middle. Season with the salt. Knead the potatoes and flour together until it's a smooth ball of dough that's slightly sticky. If the dough is too sticky, add more of the remaining ½ cup flour gradually to achieve the smooth consistency.

Divide the dough into 4 equal pieces and cover 3 of them with a dampened kitchen towel. Roll the uncovered piece of dough into a 1"-thick rope. Cut into ¾" pieces. Turn a fork over and hold at a 45-degree angle, with the tines touching the work surface. Working with one piece of dough at a time, roll it down the fork tines, pressing with your thumb to make ridges on one side. Place on a large baking sheet lined with a kitchen towel. Repeat with the remaining pieces of dough.

Bring a large pot of salted water to a boil. Add half the gnocchi and cook until they bob to the surface of the water. Transfer to a shallow bowl and cook the remaining gnocchi. Serve with the Meat Ragu (page 134).

Per serving: *393 calories, 17 g protein, 59 g carbohydrates, 9 g total fat, 3 g saturated fat, 4 g fiber, 499 mg sodium*

SPAGHETTI WITH WILTED ARUGULA, MASCARPONE, AND LIME

8 ounces spaghetti

2 tablespoons mascarpone

2 limes, one zested and juiced, the other quartered

$^1/_8$ teaspoon kosher salt

Freshly ground black pepper

3 ounces baby arugula

Red-pepper flakes

2 tablespoons crushed toasted hazelnuts (see page 100)

If you have pasta on hand, you have dinner. That was the case when Tom and I created this dish, which has become one of our favorites. It was a necessity-is-the-mother-of-invention moment: We were hungry, and there was little but arugula, mascarpone cheese, and limes in the refrigerator.

FILL A LARGE pot with generously salted water and bring to a boil. Add the spaghetti and cook according to package directions. Reserve ¾ cup of the cooking water, then drain the pasta in a colander. Return the noodles to the pot.

Meanwhile, combine the mascarpone, lime zest, juice, and salt and pepper to taste in a large bowl. Add ¼ cup of the pasta water and whisk until smooth and creamy. Add the sauce to the noodles and toss well to incorporate. Taste and adjust the seasonings. Add the arugula to the pasta and toss to thoroughly incorporate. Thin with a little of the remaining pasta water, if necessary. Garnish with the pepper flakes and hazelnuts. Serve warm, garnished with lime wedges.

Per serving: 310 calories, 10 g protein, 46 g carbohydrates, 10 g total fat, 4 g saturated fat, 3 g fiber, 75 mg sodium

Fusilli with Garlicky Broccoli

I based this recipe on the classic spaghetti *aglio e olio*, spaghetti in garlic and olive oil, a dish every Italian knows how to make. Adding broccoli was this desperate mother's attempt to sneak vegetables into her son's dinner whenever possible. It worked! Occasionally, I toss a cut-up chicken breast into the mix to make it slightly heartier.

FILL A LARGE pot with generously salted water and bring to a boil. Add the pasta and cook according to package directions. After 4 minutes, toss the broccoli into the pot. Reserve 1 cup of the cooking water, then drain the pasta and broccoli in a colander.

Meanwhile, heat the oil in a large skillet over very low heat. Add the garlic and sauté just until it begins to sizzle (do not let it brown). Turn the garlic and continue to cook, 1 to 2 minutes. Add the salt, pepper, paprika, pepper flakes, and salt and black pepper to taste, and stir to arrest the browning. If the garlic appears to be coloring, stir it sooner. Continue to cook until the smaller pieces of garlic become golden. Turn off the heat and set the skillet aside.

Once the pasta and broccoli are cooked, turn the heat on under the skillet to medium-low. Add the pasta and toss to thoroughly combine with the oil and garlic. Season to taste with the salt and pepper. Moisten the pasta, if necessary, with the reserved pasta water. Garnish with cheese and serve immediately.

Per serving: *550 calories, 17 g protein, 78 g carbohydrates, 21 g total fat, 3 g saturated fat, 8 g fiber, 139 mg sodium*

YIELD
Serves 4

- 12 ounces fusilli
- 2 pounds broccoli, trimmed into florets, stems peeled and sliced
- $1/3$ cup extra-virgin olive oil
- 15–20 cloves garlic, smashed
- $1/4$ teaspoon paprika
- $1/4$ teaspoon red-pepper flakes
- $1/8$ teaspoon kosher salt
- Freshly ground black pepper
- Grated Parmigiano-Reggiano cheese

PASTA ALLE VONGOLE

YIELD
Serves 4–6

2 tablespoons extra-virgin olive oil

3 cloves garlic, minced

$1/8$ teaspoon red-pepper flakes

$1/3$ cup dry white wine

3–4 dozen littleneck clams, scrubbed well, broken or cracked clams discarded

$1/4$ teaspoon dried oregano

Kosher salt and freshly ground black pepper

1 pound linguine

$1/2$ cup loosely packed fresh flat-leaf parsley leaves, chopped

You cannot beat the simplicity and flavor of a good pasta with white clam sauce, but the clams must be ultra-fresh—straight from the fish market. My mother always served this with football-size loaves of crusty Italian bread when I was growing up. I limit myself now to one slice—and savor every minute of using it to soak up the briny sauce.

HEAT THE OIL In a large sauté pan with a tight-fitting lid, over medium-low heat. Add the garlic and pepper flakes and sauté until fragrant. Don't let the garlic brown!

Add the white wine and clams, increase the heat to high, and cover the pan. Cook, stirring occasionally, until all of the clams have opened, about 15 minutes. As the clams open, transfer them to a large bowl and cover with foil. When all of the clams are removed, reduce the heat to medium-low, add the oregano, cover, and bring to a simmer. Season to taste with salt and pepper. It's not unusual to not need any salt.

Meanwhile, bring a large pot of generously salted water to a boil. Cook the linguine according to package directions. Using tongs, transfer the linguine to the sauté pan with the clam juice and toss to coat. Turn off the heat and add the clams and any juices that have collected in the bowl. Using tongs, turn the linguine to coat it with the sauce. Top with parsley. Serve immediately.

Per serving (when serving 4): *556 calories, 26 g protein, 88 g carbohydrates, 9 g total fat, 1.5 g saturated fat, 4 g fiber, 115 mg sodium*

Per serving (when serving 6): *370 calories, 17 g protein, 59 g carbohydrates, 6 g total fat, 1 g saturated fat, 3 g fiber, 77 mg sodium*

LASAGNA ALLA BESCIAMELLA

I may have grown up in an Italian-American family, but the idea of using besciamella, a white sauce, in lasagna never occurred to me until Tom and I visited Tenuta Torciano, a charming vineyard just outside the enchanting walled town of San Gimignano in Tuscany. After tasting the lasagna there, I instantly felt compelled to change my mother's and Nonnie's recipe (with lots of mozzarella and red meat sauce)—the first dish my mother taught me how to make—forever. We went to the vineyard's restaurant twice, and the second time Pierluigi brought out extra because he knew Tom would eat it! Now I do as those Italians do and layer the unctuous sauce into the stacks. I like using no-cook noodles because the edges don't shrink.

YIELD

Serves 8–10

1½ quarts Meat Ragu (page 134)

12 oven-ready lasagna noodles (from one 16-ounce package)

2½ cups Besciamella (page 134)

2¼ cups finely grated Parmigiano-Reggiano cheese

PREHEAT THE OVEN to 350°F. Spread an even layer of the Meat Ragu sauce over the bottom of a 9" x 13" baking dish. Arrange 3 lasagna noodles over the sauce. Avoid overlapping or allowing them to touch the sides of the pan because they will expand as they cook. Press down slightly to let the sauce spread around them. Cover with one-quarter of the Besciamella and sprinkle with ²/₃ cup of the cheese. Repeat with another layer of ragu, noodles (pressing down slightly on the noodles), Besciamella, and cheese, and repeat one more time. Over the final layer of noodles, spread the remaining Besciamella and ragu.

Cover the pan with foil and bake until heated through, about 35 minutes. Remove the foil and continue baking until the top is brown and bubbling, about 20 minutes more. During the last 10 minutes of baking, scatter the remaining ¼ cup cheese all over. Let the lasagna stand for 10 minutes before serving.

Per serving (when serving 8): *514 calories, 29 g protein, 35 g carbohydrates, 26 g total fat, 12 g saturated fat, 3 g fiber, 987 mg sodium*

Per serving (when serving 10): *411 calories, 23 g protein, 28 g carbohydrates, 21 g total fat, 10 g saturated fat, 2 g fiber, 790 mg sodium*

(continued)

MEAT RAGU

YIELD

Makes 2 quarts

3 tablespoons extra-virgin olive oil

1 yellow onion, finely chopped

2 cloves garlic, pushed through a press

1 pound ground beef

4 links sweet Italian sausage, casings removed

1 teaspoon kosher salt

1 teaspoon dried oregano

Freshly ground black pepper

1 1/2 cups dry white wine

2 boxes (26.5 ounces each) Pomi strained tomatoes

This is Nonnie's recipe, passed on to my mother, then on to me, and now on to you. I promise you neither of them left out an ingredient, as Italian cooks are known to do. Double the ingredients to make a big batch and freeze some in containers with tight-fitting lids.

HEAT THE OIL in a large saucepan over medium-low heat. Add the onion and garlic and sauté until soft and fragrant, about 8 minutes. Add the ground beef, sausage, salt, oregano, and pepper to taste and increase the heat to high. Cook, breaking up the meat with a wooden spoon, until it is browned all over. Add the wine and bring to a boil. Boil 2 minutes, then add the tomatoes and return the mixture to a boil. Reduce the heat and simmer, partially covered, until the sauce thickens and flavors come together, about 1 hour.

Per cup: 292 calories, 20 g protein, 11 g carbohydrates, 16 g total fat, 5 g saturated fat, 2 g fiber, 790 mg sodium

BESCIAMELLA

YIELD

Makes about 2 1/2 cups

1 1/2 cups whole milk

4 tablespoons (1/2 stick) unsalted butter

1/4 cup all-purpose flour

1/8 teaspoon nutmeg

Kosher salt and freshly ground white pepper

HEAT THE MILK in a small saucepan over medium heat until just simmering, then turn off the heat. Meanwhile, melt the butter in a medium heavy-bottomed saucepan over medium-high heat. Add the flour and cook, whisking constantly, until the mixture thickens and then loosens again, about 2 minutes. Add the hot milk, whisking constantly. Bring to a boil. Add the nutmeg and salt and pepper to taste. Reduce the heat to low and continue to cook, whisking almost constantly, for 2 minutes. Remove from the heat and use immediately.

Per 1/2 cup: 149 calories, 3 g protein, 8 g carbohydrates, 12 g total fat, 7 g saturated fat, 0 g fiber, 80 mg sodium

CLASSIC SHRIMP SCAMPI

I know. Who needs another recipe for scampi? I felt compelled to include it for two reasons: Shrimp is the only shellfish I could ever get Wolfie to eat, and it never hurts to remind you just how *easy* it is to put a delicious, gorgeous dinner on the table, especially during the week.

BRING A 6- to 8-quart soup pot of generously salted water to a boil.

Meanwhile, heat the oil in a large sauté pan over high heat until shimmering. Season the shrimp all over with salt and pepper. Add the shrimp to the pan in one layer and cook for 1 minute. Turn and cook 1 minute more. Using a slotted spoon, transfer the shrimp to a bowl.

Add the garlic and shallot to the pan and cook for 1 minute. Add the wine, lemon juice, pepper flakes, and oregano and simmer for 3 minutes. Whisk in the butter piece by piece, thoroughly incorporating each piece before adding the next. Taste and season with additional salt and pepper as needed. Add the shrimp back to the pan and simmer until completely cooked through, about 2 minutes. Stir in the parsley. Remove the skillet from the heat.

Add the capellini to the boiling water and cook until just tender, about 3 minutes. Reserve 1 cup of the cooking water and transfer the capellini to a colander to drain. Toss the capellini with the shrimp and parsley, adding some of the pasta water, if necessary, to keep it moist. Serve warm with crusty bread.

Per serving: *656 calories, 33 g protein, 74 g carbohydrates, 22 g total fat, 9 g saturated fat, 3 g fiber, 376 mg sodium*

YIELD
Serves 4

2 tablespoons extra-virgin olive oil

2 pounds large shrimp (16–20 count), peeled and deveined

Kosher salt and freshly ground black pepper

12 cloves garlic, finely chopped

1 shallot, finely chopped

1 cup dry white wine

$^{1}/_{4}$ cup freshly squeezed lemon juice (from 1 to $1^{1}/_{2}$ lemons)

Pinch red-pepper flakes (optional)

Pinch dried oregano

4 tablespoons ($^{1}/_{2}$ stick) unsalted butter, cut up

$^{3}/_{4}$ cup loosely packed fresh flat-leaf parsley leaves, chopped

12 ounces capellini

Crusty bread

MOM'S SPAGHETTI AND MEATBALLS

YIELD
Serves 12

1 pound ground beef

1 pound ground pork

2 eggs, lightly beaten

1 cup Italian-style dried bread crumbs

10 cloves garlic, half pushed through a press, the other half sliced

1³/₄ cups finely grated Pecorino Romano cheese

1¹/₄ teaspoons kosher salt

Freshly ground black pepper

¹/₂ cup extra-virgin olive oil

1 yellow onion, finely chopped

1 cup dry white wine

2 boxes (26.5 ounces each) Pomi strained tomatoes

¹/₄ teaspoon dried oregano

15 fresh basil leaves plus more, cut into thin strips, garnish with remaining strips

Balsamic vinegar (optional)

1 teaspoon sugar (optional)

2 pounds spaghetti

More than any other recipe, this one reminds me of my mother, who was *always* in the kitchen. In fact, to her, it was like being at the office, doing a job she thoroughly loved. And she sprinkled that love into every meal she served.

COMBINE THE BEEF, pork, eggs, bread crumbs, the pressed garlic, ¹/₄ cup of the cheese, ¹/₂ teaspoon of the salt, and pepper to taste in a large bowl. Using your hands, thoroughly mix the ingredients together until evenly incorporated. Roll into meatballs slightly larger than golf balls, setting them on baking sheets as you work.

Heat the oil over medium heat in a large Dutch oven until it shimmers. Working in batches and taking care not to crowd the pan, sauté the meatballs, turning frequently, until browned on all sides, about 5 minutes. Using a slotted spoon, transfer them from the pan to a second baking sheet.

Reduce the heat to medium-low, add the onion to the pan, and sauté, stirring occasionally, until fragrant, about 2 minutes. Add the sliced garlic, stir, and cook for 1 minute more. Add the wine, increase the heat, and bring to a boil, then reduce the heat and simmer for 2 minutes. Add the tomatoes, oregano, 4 of the basil leaves, the remaining ³/₄ teaspoon salt, and the meatballs along with any juices that have accumulated on the plate. Simmer, partially covered, until the flavors come together, about 1 hour 20 minutes. Taste and adjust the seasonings. If additional brightness is desired, add some vinegar; for sweetness, some sugar; and for deeper tomato flavor, more salt.

Meanwhile, cook the spaghetti in two batches in boiling salted water (3 tablespoons salt for 6 quarts of water) according to package directions. Drain and serve with the meatballs and sauce ladled on top. Garnish with the basil strips and pass the remaining Pecorino Romano.

Per serving: *699 calories, 31 g protein, 70 g carbohydrates, 29 g total fat, 11 g saturated fat, 4 g fiber, 750 mg sodium*

I Love the Way
You Look

AND I MEAN MY plate of pasta! So much of the pleasure that comes from eating almost anything is in the presentation. As a friend of mine likes to say, eat with your eyes first. To create a great beehive-shaped mound of pasta on the plate like so many chefs do, plunge a pair of tongs into the pot of pasta, grabbing some of the strands with it, and start twirling until there's a serving size amount of the linguine on the tongs. Slide it off onto a plate or into a shallow bowl. I find that when I serve pasta this way, I tend to eat less because the presentation looks so hefty.

CHICKEN PAILLARD WITH SALSA VERDE

YIELD

Serves 4

4 chicken cutlets (4 ounces each)

Kosher salt and freshly ground black pepper

1 egg, lightly beaten

$^1/_2$ cup panko bread crumbs

Lemon wedges

Salsa Verde (below)

This is Tom's brilliant answer to a lower-fat version of the classic Italian preparation of a chicken cutlet: coated in bread crumbs and fried in oil. He used light-as-a-feather panko bread crumbs, then grilled the cutlet. It's delicious with a good squeeze of lemon and a little salsa verde or with a lightly dressed arugula salad served on top.

COAT A GRILL rack with oil and preheat the grill on high for about 5 minutes.

Meanwhile, place a cutlet between two pieces of plastic wrap and, using a rolling pin or the flat side of a meat pounder, pound it to about $^1/_4$" thickness. Season all over with salt and pepper. Repeat with the remaining cutlets.

Whisk the egg in a large shallow bowl. Spread the panko in another large shallow bowl. Have a large tray ready. Dip one cutlet in the egg to coat all over, letting the excess drip off, and dredge in the panko, coating well. Set aside on the tray and repeat with the remaining cutlets. Refrigerate cutlets for 20 minutes.

Grill the chicken over direct heat on medium-high until cooked through, about 2 minutes per side. Garnish with the lemon wedges and serve with the Salsa Verde.

SALSA VERDE

YIELD

Makes 1$^1/_2$ cups

$^1/_4$ cup extra-virgin olive oil

Grated zest of 1 lemon

$^1/_4$ cup freshly squeezed lemon juice

2 cups fresh flat-leaf parsley

2 anchovy fillets

2 cloves garlic

2 tablespoons capers, rinsed

Freshly ground black pepper

COMBINE THE OIL, lemon zest, lemon juice, parsley, anchovies, garlic, capers, and pepper to taste in a food processor and pulse until smooth. Transfer to a small bowl and serve.

Per serving: *369 calories, 36 g protein, 10 g carbohydrates, 21 g total fat, 4 g saturated fat, 2 g fiber, 398 mg sodium*

EDDIE'S FAVORITE CHICKEN SAMBAL

YIELD
Serves 4

1½ pounds boneless, skinless chicken thighs

Kosher salt and freshly ground black pepper

2 tablespoons peanut oil

2 onions, halved and thinly sliced

4 cloves garlic, thinly sliced

1 tablespoon grated fresh galangal or ginger

½ cup chopped tomato

2 tablespoons sambal oelek

2 tablespoons less sodium soy sauce

1 tablespoon light brown sugar

2 tablespoons freshly squeezed lemon juice

2 cups cooked white rice

1 tablespoon fish sauce

1 cup chopped fresh cilantro leaves

This is the dish that Ed's mother and I bonded over. Very early in our relationship, Mrs. Van Halen took me into her kitchen and showed me how to make this Indonesian classic. Not only had I already fallen in love with her son, but from that point on, I was in love with her! Sambal oelek is a very spicy chile-based condiment available in specialty food shops and some grocery stores.

SEASON THE CHICKEN all over with salt and pepper. Heat 1 tablespoon of the oil in a large skillet over medium-high heat until shimmering. Add the chicken and brown well, about 6 minutes on each side. Don't worry if the chicken sticks and tears a little as you flip it. Transfer the chicken, which will not be fully cooked, to a plate.

Heat the remaining 1 tablespoon oil in the skillet. Add the onions, garlic, galangal, tomato, and sambal oelek and cook until fragrant, about 2 minutes. Combine the soy sauce, brown sugar, lemon juice, fish sauce, and ¼ cup water in a small cup and stir. Pour into the skillet and, using a wooden spoon, stir up any browned bits from the bottom of the skillet.

Add the chicken back to the skillet, along with any juices that have accumulated on the plate. Cover the pan and simmer until the chicken is cooked through, about 4 minutes. Transfer the chicken from the skillet to a cutting board and cut each piece of chicken into thirds. Arrange over rice and spoon the sauce over. Garnish with the cilantro and serve.

Per serving: *316 calories, 36 g protein, 14 g carbohydrates, 14 g total fat, 3 g saturated fat, 1 g fiber, 1,043 mg sodium*

CHICKEN WITH PRUNES AND OLIVES

Years ago, my friend Suzanne turned me on to Chicken Marbella, the Silver Palate classic. Since then, I've flavored the dish to suit my own tastes—with extra prunes and garlic-stuffed olives. When Wolfie wasn't around, I'd skip the drumsticks. There are times when all I have on hand are boneless chicken breasts, in which case I cut the cooking time. If you need to get dinner on the table fast, let the chicken marinate at room temperature while the oven preheats.

COMBINE THE OIL, vinegar, prunes, olives, capers, garlic, bay leaves, oregano, and salt and pepper to taste in a large shallow baking dish. Add the chicken and turn to coat. Cover with plastic wrap and marinate at least 1 hour or overnight.

Preheat the oven to 375°F. Using a slotted spoon, remove the chicken from the marinade to a plate. Pour the marinade into a 9" x 13" baking dish. Arrange the chicken on top, skin side up. Sprinkle the brown sugar over the chicken and pour the white wine around them.

Bake, basting three or four times with the pan juices, until the chicken is crispy on top and cooked through, 1 hour to 1 hour 20 minutes.

Transfer the chicken, prunes, olives, and capers to a serving platter. Moisten with a few spoonfuls of the pan juices and sprinkle generously with the parsley or cilantro. Pour the remaining pan juices into a sauceboat and pass with the chicken.

Per serving: *650 calories, 41 g protein, 48 g carbohydrates, 31 g total fat, 5 g saturated fat, 4 g fiber, 792 mg sodium*

YIELD
Serves 6

²/₃ cup extra-virgin olive oil

²/₃ cup red wine vinegar

2 cups pitted prunes

20 garlic-stuffed olives

¼ cup capers with a bit of juice

10 cloves garlic, pushed through a press

2 bay leaves

2 tablespoons dried oregano

¼ teaspoon kosher salt

Freshly ground black pepper

3 pounds bone-in chicken breasts, skin removed

¼ cup light brown sugar

½ cup white wine

½ cup fresh flat-leaf parsley or cilantro leaves, finely chopped

THE DINNER PARTY

WOLFIE WAS 5 YEARS old when I hosted my first official dinner party, the kind that my mother used to throw without seeming rushed or worried. I was not as calm as I remember her. I was not nervous, either. I'm not wired that way. But I wanted the meal to be nice and my house to feel warm and inviting, the usual concerns of a hostess. The party was for the women in my book club. There were 8 of us. We knew each other through our children, who were beginning school together. Wolfie's 21st birthday has come and gone, so you get an idea of how long ago this was.

Like most book clubs, we alternated between each other's homes, and whoever hosted was charged with picking the book and making dinner. I had chosen *Angela's Ashes*, Frank McCourt's wonderful memoir about surviving his miserable childhood in Limerick, Ireland. I didn't have much experience entertaining other than having family and friends over to watch football or celebrate birthdays. My then-husband, Ed, was on tour, so I was on my own. I went out and bought new place mats and fresh flowers. I wanted the dining room table to look beautiful without being overdone. I had the same goal for my meal.

I made Chicken with Prunes and Olives (page 141), a delicious baked chicken with green olives (my favorite), white wine, prunes, capers, and other goodies. It's easy, gorgeous, and scrumptious. It baked for about an hour, but it required frequent basting. I tried to time it with my guests' arrivals, so I was cooking up to the last minute. I was also reading the last 30 pages of the book. It was a race till the doorbell rang. I remember taking the chicken out of the oven, transferring it to a favorite serving platter, and then marveling at the easy way the rest of the evening unfolded. The food was a hit, and the conversation even better.

Since then, my book club dinners have become opportunities to experiment with a variety of dishes and ingredients. Concerns about entertaining disappeared ages ago. Now I focus on food and friendship. If I'm having good friends over, I know the party will be a success, and so I concentrate on the menu. Seasonality determines what I'm going to make. I peruse some favorite cookbooks but don't force the issue. I look at what's available. That can answer so many questions. In the winter, I serve soups and stews. In the summer, I find myself thinking about lighter, cleaner courses, like chilled, crisp salad; vegetables cooked al dente and dusted with herbs, salt, and pepper; and salmon.

After more than a decade and a half of these dinners, we have shared each other's lives. Our children are graduating from college. Along the way, our tastes have also changed. Whereas 10 years ago a table might have been filled with serving bowls and sauces, we have learned to appreciate the elegant simplicity of, say, lamb chops accompanied by spinach and roasted potatoes with a sprig of rosemary. Food and life are one and the same: Over time you learn that the essentials are all that really matter.

My brother Pat and his wife Stacy share an al fresco meal with us.

Thursday Turkey Meat Loaf

YIELD

Serves 6–8

2 slices soft white sandwich bread, torn into small pieces (about 2 cups)

$1/2$ cup whole milk

$1^1/_2$ pounds ground turkey

2 large eggs, lightly beaten

$3/4$ cup grated Parmigiano-Reggiano cheese

8 thin slices pancetta (about 4 ounces), finely chopped

$1/2$ onion, finely chopped

3 cloves garlic, pushed through a press

$1/4$ cup plus 1 tablespoon ketchup

1 cup loosely packed fresh flat-leaf parsley leaves, chopped

$1/2$ teaspoon dried oregano

$1/4$ cup Italian-style dried bread crumbs

$1/4$ teaspoon kosher salt

Freshly ground black pepper

The memory is so vivid: I'm standing at the kitchen counter, mixing bread crumbs, onions, ground turkey, cheese, eggs, and seasonings while Wolfie sits at the kitchen table doing his homework. They're some of the fondest memories I have of his childhood—and I'm certain half of America can relate to this scene. Back then, I relied on a repeated weekly menu, which is how this meat loaf earned its name. It makes excellent sandwiches the day after it is baked.

PREHEAT THE OVEN to 500°F. Combine the bread and milk in a large bowl and soak for 10 minutes. Add the turkey, eggs, cheese, pancetta, onion, garlic, 1 tablespoon of the ketchup, the parsley, oregano, dried bread crumbs, and salt and pepper to taste. Mix well with your hands.

Shape into an 8" x 5" loaf and transfer to a rimmed baking sheet. Bake for 15 minutes. Reduce the heat to 325°F and slather the remaining $1/4$ cup ketchup all over the top of the loaf. Bake until a meat thermometer inserted in the center of the loaf reads 165°F, about 45 minutes. Let the meat loaf rest for 10 minutes, then transfer to a platter and serve.

Per serving (when serving 6): *378 calories, 32 g protein, 14 g carbohydrates, 21 g total fat, 7 g saturated fat, 1 g fiber, 1,008 mg sodium*

Per serving (when serving 8): *283 calories, 24 g protein, 11 g carbohydrates, 16 g total fat, 6 g saturated fat, 1 g fiber, 756 mg sodium*

QUICHE VALERIE

I made *a lot* of quiche in the '80s, just like everyone else. I was newly married to Ed, and when I whipped one of these out of the oven, it looked like I knew my way around a kitchen! I took a break from quiche for a while—like most everyone who overindulged back then—but it's back in my repertoire, the perfect catchall for what's left in the fridge. I won't wag a finger at you for using a prepared crust, but if you're going to do that, buy the best you can find.

YIELD
Serves 6–8

½ recipe Mom's Flaky Pie Dough (page 210)

1 tablespoon extra-virgin olive oil

2 tablespoons chopped onion, shallots, or scallions

1 cup small mushrooms, sliced

3 large eggs, lightly beaten

½ cup light cream

2 tablespoons chopped fresh herbs, such as basil, parsley, mint, chives, or tarragon

2 tablespoons grated hard cheese, such as Manchego, Pecorino Romano, Parmigiano-Reggiano, or Gruyère; or 3 tablespoons crumbled soft cheese, such as blue, goat, or feta

¼ teaspoon kosher salt

¼ teaspoon nutmeg

Freshly ground black pepper

1 cup cooked veggies, such as spinach, broccoli, or asparagus

ON A WELL-FLOURED surface and using a well-floured rolling pin, roll out the pie dough into a 9" to 10" round. Lightly flour the pin as needed to prevent sticking. If the dough tends to stay sticky, refrigerate until firm and begin again, or use a large flat spatula or bench scraper to transfer the dough to an 8" pie plate and press into shape. Refrigerate the pie shell for 20 minutes.

Meanwhile, preheat the oven to 350°F. Place a sheet of parchment paper or foil into the pie shell and fill with pie weights, raw rice, or dried beans. Bake until the edges are lightly golden, about 15 minutes. Remove the paper and weights, and bake until golden and cooked on the bottom and sides, about 15 minutes more. Remove the piecrust but keep the oven on.

While the crust is baking, heat the oil in a medium skillet over medium-low heat. Add the onion and sauté until soft and translucent, stirring occasionally, about 8 minutes. Add the mushrooms and cook until well browned and cooked through, stirring occasionally, 10 minutes.

Combine the eggs, cream, herbs, cheese, salt, nutmeg, and pepper to taste in a large bowl and lightly whisk. Stir in the vegetables and mushroom mixture. Pour the mixture into the crust and bake until set, about 45 minutes. Let cool for 15 minutes. Cut into wedges and serve.

Per serving (when serving 6): *310 calories, 8 g protein, 22 g carbohydrates, 22 g total fat, 12 g saturated fat, 2 g fiber, 394 mg sodium*

Per serving (when serving 8): *232 calories, 6 g protein, 16 g carbohydrates, 16 g total fat, 9 g saturated fat, 1 g fiber, 295 mg sodium*

Mrs. Van Halen's Bami Goreng

YIELD

Serves 6

QUICKIE KETJAP SAMBAL

½ cup packed light brown sugar

½ cup less sodium soy sauce

3 whole pieces star anise, ground in a spice grinder (about 1 teaspoon), optional

3 cloves garlic, pushed through a press

1 thumb-size knob fresh ginger, peeled and grated

¾ jalapeño chile pepper, seeded and sliced (wear plastic gloves when handling)

STIR-FRY

8 ounces spaghetti

¼ cup peanut oil

8 ounces turkey breast, cut into bite-size pieces

8 ounces boneless pork chop, cut into bite-size pieces

1 onion, chopped

12 ounces green cabbage, shredded

1 teaspoon (or more) sambal oelek or Sriracha

¼ cup chopped fresh cilantro (optional)

I was lucky enough to get to spend time in the kitchen with Eddie's mother, Eugenia, long enough to learn some of her specialty dishes. Her Indonesian and Dutch heritage came through strongest in her cooking. I have fond memories of watching her toss a bit of this and a bit of that into a pan to make her *ketjap sambal*, an Indonesian soy sauce similar to sweet soy sauce that was to the Van Halen household what ketchup was to mine. Mrs. VH spiced hers up with jalapeño peppers because her boys liked things spicy. The prepared version is not all that easy to find, but you can put together a version of it from supermarket ingredients. The sambal oelek, a chili paste that contains no additional flavorings or spices, is available at specialty and gourmet food stores. In a pinch, you can use a supermarket chili paste or Sriracha, which I use.

TO MAKE THE QUICKIE KETJAP SAMBAL: Combine the brown sugar, soy sauce, star anise, garlic, ginger, chile pepper, and ⅓ cup water in a medium saucepan and stir. Cook over medium heat until the mixture is thick enough to coat the back of a spoon, about 22 minutes. Remove and discard the star anise and set the ketjap aside.

TO MAKE THE STIR-FRY: Bring a large pot of salted water to a boil. Cook the spaghetti in the boiling water according to package directions, stirring once or twice. Drain well and spread on a clean kitchen towel to dry out. Preheat a wok or large skillet over high heat and swirl in 2 tablespoons of the oil. Fry the spaghetti, in batches if necessary, until they begin to brown and crisp up in some places. Using tongs, remove them to a plate and set aside.

Swirl 1½ teaspoons of the oil into the wok. Add half of the turkey and pork and cook, stirring occasionally, until well browned all over. Transfer to a separate bowl. Heat another 1½ teaspoons of the oil in the wok and repeat with the remaining meat. Transfer to the same bowl. Add the onion to the wok and cook, stirring once or twice, until fragrant, about 1 minute. Add the cabbage and sambal oelek (or more to taste) and stir to combine, about 30 seconds.

Add one-fourth of the ketjap sambal mixed with $\frac{1}{4}$ cup water and cook, covered, until the cabbage is slightly wilted, about 3 minutes. Add the meats back to the wok and cook, stirring, for 1 minute. Add the spaghetti to the mixture and toss until the ingredients are evenly distributed and the pasta is warmed through. Transfer to a warm serving platter, garnish with the cilantro (if using), and serve with the remaining ketjap sambal.

Per serving: *434 calories, 24 g protein, 54 g carbohydrates, 14 g total fat, 3 g saturated fat, 3 g fiber, 969 mg sodium*

Peppered Beef Tenderloin with Horseradish Sauce

As a teenager, Tom worked at his aunt and uncle's restaurant. That's where his cousin Dennis taught him how to properly roast a tenderloin more than two decades ago. Whenever he wants to impress someone, Tom turns to it. Believe me, it works! Ask your butcher to tie a 12- to 18-inch-long prime cut of beef. It's okay if it's uneven in thickness; the thinner parts will cook to medium and the remaining to medium-rare. If you don't own a meat thermometer, now is the time to get one.

PREHEAT THE OVEN to 450°F.

TO MAKE THE SAUCE: Whisk together the sour cream, mustard, and horseradish in a small bowl until smooth. The sauce can be prepared 2 days in advance, covered, and refrigerated until ready to serve.

TO MAKE THE BEEF: Coarsely grind the peppercorns in a spice or coffee grinder. Transfer them to a medium bowl. Whisk in the salt, mustard, butter, and parsley until thoroughly combined. Rub the spiced butter all over the tenderloin, rolling the beef in the portions that fall off to coat completely. The beef can be prepared up to this point, covered, and refrigerated 1 day in advance.

Place the beef on a rack and set in a shallow baking pan. Roast until a meat thermometer inserted into the center registers 130°F for medium rare, about 35 minutes. Remove from the oven and let stand for 10 minutes. Transfer the beef to a cutting board, preferably a meat board with a reservoir to catch the juices, and slice. Arrange the slices on a platter, pour the juices over, and garnish with the parsley. Serve with the sauce on the side.

Per serving (when serving 6): *434 calories, 43 g protein, 9 g carbohydrates, 24 g total fat, 11 g saturated fat, 2 g fiber, 1,480 mg sodium*

Per serving (when serving 8): *325 calories, 32 g protein, 6 g carbohydrates, 18 g total fat, 8 g saturated fat, 2 g fiber, 1,110 mg sodium*

YIELD
Serves 6–8

SAUCE

1 cup sour cream

3 tablespoons Dijon mustard

2 tablespoons prepared horseradish

BEEF

6 tablespoons mixed peppercorns (black, white, green, pink)

1 tablespoon kosher coarse salt

3 tablespoons Dijon mustard

2 tablespoons unsalted butter, at room temperature

1 cup loosely packed fresh flat-leaf parsley, finely chopped, plus additional for garnish

1–2½ pounds beef tenderloin, trimmed and tied if uneven

Pa V's Pot Roast

YIELD
Serves 8

2 pounds chuck roast

10 cloves garlic, halved

$\frac{1}{2}$ teaspoon kosher salt

Freshly ground black pepper

1 tablespoon extra-virgin olive oil

3 carrots, cut into large bite-size chunks

2 onions, thickly sliced

2 bay leaves

4 cups dry white wine

I love Tom's dad, a Sicilian man with a love of his wife's simple, home-cooked Italian food. He's got a little fire in him, and it revealed itself one night when they were visiting and the talk turned to dinner. He managed to turn a humble piece of chuck roast into what was the most gloriously lacquered, juicy piece of meat I'd had in a long time. Yes, he had me at this pot roast, which requires little more than making lots of slits in it for stuffing whole garlic cloves, searing it, and then walking away as it roasts in the oven.

The first time we tried to replicate it, the power went out right after the searing step. No problem. Tom set the pan over two burners on the gas stove, lit it up, and 5 hours and many splashes of wine later, we had an unexpectedly romantic dinner by lots of candlelight. Tom's Green Beans with Shallots (page 175) makes a nice side dish here.

PREHEAT THE OVEN to 300°F. With the tip of a paring knife, make ten $\frac{3}{4}$"-deep slits on each side of the roast. Insert a garlic clove half into each slit. Season the meat all over with the salt and pepper to taste. Heat the oil in a Dutch oven over medium heat until shimmering. Gently set the roast in it and sear all over, turning with tongs, until well browned, about 14 minutes. Remove the meat from the pan to a plate.

Add the carrots, onions, and bay leaves to the pan and cook for 2 minutes. Add the wine and bring to a boil. Reduce the heat and simmer, stirring up the crispy bits at the bottom of the pan with a wooden spoon. Return the roast to the pot, laying it on top of the vegetables. Cover and roast for 1 hour 30 minutes. Flip the meat over, cover, and cook until fork-tender, 45 minutes to 1 hour 30 minutes more, depending on the thickness of the roast.

Remove the roast and vegetables to a platter. Season the meat with additional salt to taste. Pour the sauce through a strainer into a gravy boat and pass with the meat and vegetables.

Per serving: *288 calories, 26 g protein, 9 g carbohydrates, 7 g total fat, 2 g saturated fat, 1 g fiber, 221 mg sodium*

Express Beef Bourguignon

I once made a version of this classic French stew that took 2 days. I knew there had to be a better way. Granted, it was delicious, but I've never had the luxury of that kind of time to cook since. This quickie version is great for bringing to book club or when my in-laws are visiting. Serve the stew over buttered and parsleyed potatoes or noodles, and open a nice Cabernet Sauvignon.

COOK THE BACON in a large Dutch oven over medium heat until crisp. Using a slotted spoon, remove the bacon to a paper towel-lined plate. If there's scant bacon fat in the pot, add the olive oil and set aside. Place the flour in a shallow bowl. Season the beef well with the salt and pepper to taste, then toss it in the flour to coat, shaking off the excess flour. Heat the oil until shimmering and brown the beef in three batches. Transfer the browned pieces to a large bowl.

Add the mushrooms to the pan and cook until browned well, about 4 minutes. If the pan looks dry, add the olive oil at this stage (or add more, if the oil was already added above). Push the mushrooms to the sides of the pan, add the onion, and cook until fragrant, about 1 minute. Add the celery, whole carrots, bay leaves, and tomato paste and cook, stirring for 2 minutes. Add the red wine, increase the heat, and bring to a boil. Then reduce the heat and simmer 2 minutes, stirring up the browned bits stuck to the bottom of the pan with a wooden spoon. Add the broth, thyme, and 1 cup water and return the meat to the pan. Simmer gently, partially covered, 1 hour. Fish out the carrots and discard.

Add the carrot chunks and pearl onions to the pot and cook until the carrots are soft and the meat is very tender when pierced with a fork, about 45 minutes more. Fish out and discard the bay leaves and celery. Season to taste with salt and pepper. Scatter the crisped bacon over the top of the stew.

Per serving: *521 calories, 34 g protein, 20 g carbohydrates, 29 g total fat, 10 g saturated fat, 3 g fiber, 445 mg sodium*

YIELD

Serves 8

4 slices bacon, cut into 1/2" pieces

1 tablespoon extra-virgin olive oil (if needed)

3 tablespoons all-purpose flour

3 pounds stew beef

1/2 teaspoon kosher salt

Freshly ground black pepper

10 ounces cremini mushrooms, halved or quartered if large

1 onion, halved and thinly sliced

2 ribs celery, cut into bite-size chunks

4 carrots, 2 whole and 2 cut into bite-size chunks

2 bay leaves

2 tablespoons tomato paste

2 cups dry red wine

1 can (14.5 ounces) reduced-sodium beef broth

2 sprigs fresh thyme or 1 teaspoon dried thyme

1 bag (16 ounces) frozen pearl onions

CHIPOTLE BISON CHEESEBURGERS

YIELD
Serves 4–6

PATTIES

1 pound ground bison

¼ teaspoon dried oregano (preferably Mexican)

¼ teaspoon kosher salt

⅛ teaspoon garlic powder

Freshly ground black pepper

SAUCE

¼ cup light sour cream

1½ chipotle chile peppers in adobo sauce, finely chopped

2 tablespoons finely chopped white onion

½ cup loosely packed fresh cilantro leaves, finely chopped

¼ teaspoon kosher salt

Freshly ground black pepper

BURGERS

4–6 whole wheat buns, split

2 tablespoons unsalted butter, softened

4–6 slices reduced-fat Cheddar cheese

1 avocado, thinly sliced

Sometimes, nothing but a grilled burger will do. I enjoyed the turkey burgers offered on the Jenny Craig program, and it pushed me to think about other lean meats I could shape into a patty and put on the grill. Bison fit the bill. Seasoned with a little oregano and garlic powder and topped with a bit of chipotle sauce, these are not your average burgers.

TO MAKE THE PATTIES: Combine the bison, oregano, salt, garlic powder, and pepper to taste in a medium bowl and mix well. Shape into patties a little more than ½" thick, place on a plate, and refrigerate for at least 1 hour.

TO MAKE THE SAUCE: Stir together the sour cream, chipotle peppers, onion, cilantro, and salt and black pepper to taste in a small bowl. Set aside.

TO MAKE THE BURGERS: Oil a grill rack and preheat the grill on high for 5 minutes. Spread the bun faces lightly with the butter. Grill the burgers over direct heat on medium-high (on a charcoal grill, set the burgers just outside the center of the grill rack), with the grill covered, for 4 minutes. Flip the burgers, top each with a slice of cheese, and grill, covered, 4 minutes more. Remove the burgers to a plate.

Grill the buns, buttered side down, over indirect heat, until golden, about 2 minutes. Set a burger on each bun bottom, top with the avocado slices and a dab of the chipotle sauce. Top with the remaining bun halves and serve.

Per serving (when serving 4): *570 calories, 32 g protein, 31 g carbohydrates, 36 g total fat, 14 g saturated fat, 7 g fiber, 783 mg sodium*

Per serving (when serving 6): *644 calories, 36 g protein, 43 g carbohydrates, 38 g total fat, 15 g saturated fat, 8 g fiber, 995 mg sodium*

WOLFIE'S MARINATED LAMB CHOPS

YIELD
Serves 4

Honestly, Wolfie and I ate these little lamb chops so often that at one point, Wolfie begged me to stop making them. But the truth is, we both loved them—and I still do. Of course, I didn't always prepare them in a marinade that required time in the refrigerator. Sometimes, a little salt and pepper was all they got. The key is to buy top-quality chops and be careful not to overcook them. Serve these with Sautéed Spinach and Mushrooms (page 169) or Tom's Green Beans with Shallots (page 171).

12 single-cut lamb chops

1 cup plain yogurt

1/4 cup freshly squeezed lime juice

4 cloves garlic, pushed through a press

1 tablespoon grated fresh ginger

1 teaspoon ground cumin

1 teaspoon turmeric

1/4 teaspoon cayenne

Pinch ground cinnamon

Pinch ground cloves

1 1/2 teaspoons kosher salt

1/4 teaspoon freshly ground black pepper

ARRANGE THE LAMB chops in a large glass baking dish and set aside. Combine the yogurt, lime juice, garlic, ginger, cumin, turmeric, cayenne, cinnamon, cloves, salt, and pepper in a bowl and stir to thoroughly combine. Pour over the chops and turn to coat them. Marinate, covered, in the refrigerator for at least 8 hours or up to 24 hours.

Coat a grill rack with oil and preheat the grill on high for 5 minutes. Reduce the heat to medium and place the chops over direct heat. Close the cover only if using a gas grill; if using a charcoal grill, leave the cover off. For medium-rare, 1" chops will take about 6 minutes per side, and 3/4" chops will take about 4 minutes per side. Remove the chops to a platter and serve.

Per serving: 330 calories, 43 g protein, 6 g carbohydrates, 14 g total fat, 5 g saturated fat, 0 g fiber, 880 mg sodium

LAMB SHEPHERD'S PIE

YIELD

Serves 6–8

1 yellow onion, finely chopped

1 rib celery, finely chopped

1 carrot, finely chopped

3 cloves garlic, pushed through
a press

1 bay leaf

1 tablespoon extra-virgin olive oil

1 pound ground lamb

3 tablespoons dry mustard

1 teaspoon kosher salt

Freshly ground black pepper

3 tablespoons tomato paste

1 tablespoon fennel seeds

$^1/_2$ cup canned tomato puree

2 tablespoons chopped fresh mint

2 tablespoons chopped fresh sage

2 pounds russet potatoes, peeled
and cut into quarters, or $2^1/_2$
cups cooked mashed potatoes

$^1/_2$ cup whole milk

3 tablespoons unsalted butter

We have turkey and mashed potatoes for Thanksgiving and then make this on the following Saturday with the leftover mashed potatoes. Lamb is a nice change from both ground beef, with which the classic version is made, and turkey, which we've eaten enough of over the previous 2 days!

PREHEAT THE OVEN to 375°F. Combine the onion, celery, carrot, garlic, bay leaf, and oil in a medium skillet (not nonstick), and cook over low heat, covered, stirring occasionally, until the vegetables are softened, about 10 minutes.

Push the vegetables to the perimeter of the pan and add the lamb. Increase the heat to high and brown the lamb all over, breaking it up with a wooden spoon. Season with the mustard, $^3/_4$ teaspoon of the salt, and pepper to taste. Stir until fragrant, about 1 minute, then add the tomato paste, fennel seeds, and tomato puree and stir again. Cook 1 minute more. Turn off the heat and stir in the mint and sage. Remove the bay leaf.

Meanwhile, put the potatoes in a medium saucepan and cover by 2" with salted water. Cover and bring to a boil. Cook until a knife releases easily from the potatoes when piercing the center, 12 to 15 minutes. Reserve 1 cup of the cooking water and drain the potatoes. In the same pot, combine the milk, butter, and $^1/_2$ cup of the cooking water and stir together over high heat. Bring to a boil.

Mash the potatoes with a masher or push through a ricer, then slowly drizzle the hot liquid over the potatoes and stir until light and fluffy. You may not need to use all of the liquid. Taste and season with pepper and the remaining $^1/_4$ teaspoon salt.

Spoon the lamb mixture into the bottom of an 8" deep-dish pie plate, spreading it evenly over the bottom of the plate. Spoon the mashed potatoes over the top, covering completely. Use the back of a spoon or an offset spatula to create a swirled pattern in the potatoes. Bake until the topping turns golden in spots, about 30 minutes. Serve warm.

Per serving (when serving 6): *431 calories, 17 g protein, 31 g carbohydrates, 27 g total fat, 12 g saturated fat, 3 g fiber, 722 mg sodium*

Per serving (when serving 8): *323 calories, 13 g protein, 23 g carbohydrates, 20 g total fat, 9 g saturated fat, 3 g fiber, 542 mg sodium*

BAKED SIDE OF SALMON WITH HONEY MUSTARD SAUCE

Serves 6–8

One 3½-pound side of wild salmon

½ cup low-fat mayonnaise

¼ cup Dijon mustard

¼ cup honey

½ cup chopped chives plus additional for garnish

Kosher salt and freshly ground white pepper

Could there be an easier way to prepare a meal that's so good for you? Think of all those omega-3s! This is one of those dishes that looks very impressive served whole, right at the table. Ask your partner or a friend to help you transfer it from the baking dish to a warmed serving platter, to prevent it from breaking or flaking before the big presentation.

PREHEAT THE OVEN to 375°F. Line a large baking sheet with parchment paper or a nonstick silicone liner, and lay the salmon, skin side down, on top. Set aside.

Combine the mayonnaise, mustard, honey, and chives in a small bowl and stir to thoroughly combine. Reserve ¾ cup of the sauce. Spoon the remaining sauce over the fish, spreading it evenly from one end to the other. Season with salt and pepper.

Roast just until the fish is opaque in the center, 20 to 30 minutes, depending on the thickness of the fish. Garnish with the chives and serve with the reserved sauce.

Per serving (when serving 6): *494 calories, 53 g protein, 15 g carbohydrates, 23 g total fat, 4 g saturated fat, 0 g fiber, 532 mg sodium*

Per serving (when serving 8): *370 calories, 40 g protein, 12 g carbohydrates, 18 g total fat, 3 g saturated fat, 0 g fiber, 400 mg sodium*

BLACKENED CATFISH TACOS

◀ YIELD ▶
Makes 8 tacos

8 tortillas, flour or corn (8" dia.)

¼ cup blackening seasoning

1 pound catfish fillets, cut into 2-ounce pieces

1 red onion, sliced into thick rings

¾ pound green cabbage, shredded

1 avocado, sliced

½ cup light sour cream

Lime wedges

1 cup loosely packed fresh cilantro leaves

Hot sauce

My parents lived in Louisiana for a short time after I left home to pursue acting. It's when I began my love affair with hot sauces and spicy ingredients in earnest. When they lived in Delaware, there was always spaghetti and meatballs on the stove, but that changed somewhat in Shreveport, where catfish was a constant. I love it blackened and tucked into a soft corn tortilla. These tacos are great for serving at a casual get-together. Lay out all the ingredients, and let everyone construct their own. Add a few more tortillas to the stack than you need—the bottom one may be charred as it warms on the grill.

COAT A GRILL rack with oil and preheat the grill on high for 5 minutes. Stack the tortillas and wrap them in foil.

Place the blackening seasoning on a dinner plate. Roll the catfish pieces in the seasoning until well coated. Reduce the grill to medium-high, and grill the fish over direct heat until cooked through, turning once, about 6 minutes. Meanwhile, grill the onion over direct heat, until well browned and wilting, turning once, about 6 minutes. At the same time, warm the tortillas in the foil over indirect heat.

Arrange the fish on a plate and transfer the onions to a separate plate. Place the cabbage, avocado, sour cream, lime wedges, and cilantro in separate bowls. Set out with the tortillas and hot sauce, and invite guests to make their own tacos.

Per serving: *300 calories, 14 g protein, 31 g carbohydrates, 13 g total fat, 3 g saturated fat, 4 g fiber, 707 mg sodium*

PAT AND STACY'S GUMBO

This classic Louisiana stew is ideal for large casual gatherings or celebrations. It takes commitment—and is always better when you make it with a few fellow cooks. The key to making great gumbo lies in the roux, flour cooked in fat to just the right color and consistency. Patience! We always serve this over cooked white rice.

TO MAKE THE STOCK: Place the turkey, onion, carrots, celery, peppercorns, and parsley in a large soup pot. Fill the pot with water to cover the ingredients by 2". Bring to a boil, reduce the heat and simmer, uncovered, 1½ hours, skimming foam off the top as necessary. Strain and discard the solids.

TO MAKE THE GUMBO: Warm the oil over medium heat until hot. Add the flour to the pan all at once, whisking until the consistency is uniform. Cook the roux, whisking occasionally, until it is the color of peanut butter, about 20 minutes. Do not let it darken any further. Gently add the celery, bell peppers, onion, scallions, and garlic to the pan, as the hot roux may spatter. Stir with a wooden spoon until the onions begin to soften, about 5 minutes.

Add about 1½ quarts of the stock, or enough to just cover the vegetables, and stir to combine. The roux may separate. Add the tomatoes with their juices, sausages, salt, black pepper, cayenne, bay leaves, and the remaining stock (about 4½ more quarts). Cover and bring to a boil, then reduce the heat and simmer 20 minutes.

Meanwhile, heat the remaining oil in a medium skillet over medium heat and add the okra. Stir and cook until the okra's gel dries out slightly, about 15 minutes. Add to the pot.

Taste the gumbo for seasoning and adjust as desired. Add the turkey or chicken chunks and serve, or simmer as long as 2 hours more to concentrate the flavors, if desired.

Per serving (when serving 25): *392 calories, 19 g protein, 38 g carbohydrates, 18 g total fat, 4 g saturated fat, 2 g fiber, 1,009 mg sodium*

Per serving (when serving 30): *327 calories, 16 g protein, 32 g carbohydrates, 15 g total fat, 3 g saturated fat, 2 g fiber, 841 mg sodium*

YIELD
Serves 25–30

STOCK
2–3 pounds skin, bones, and neck of roasted turkey or chicken

1 large white onion, quartered

2 carrots, cut into thirds

3 ribs celery, cut into thirds

2 tablespoons black peppercorns

1 cup fresh flat-leaf parsley

GUMBO
1 cup plus 2 tablespoons canola oil

1 cup all-purpose flour

6 ribs celery, chopped

3 green bell peppers, chopped

1 large white onion, chopped

1 bunch scallions, chopped

8–10 cloves garlic, chopped

2 cans (15 ounces each) diced tomatoes

12 ounces andouille sausage, sliced into ½" pieces

12 ounces smoked sausage, sliced into ½" pieces

2 tablespoons kosher salt, or more to taste

1 tablespoon freshly ground black pepper, or more to taste

1 tablespoon cayenne, or more to taste

3 bay leaves

2 10-ounce boxes frozen okra

Meat from roasted turkey or chicken, cut into bite-size chunks

15 cups white cooked rice

IT'S A GUMBO WORLD

MAKING GUMBO IS A ritual in my family. We make it when the New Orleans Saints play their first game of the season. We make it after Thanksgiving. We make it for the Super Bowl. We make it for just about any occasion that falls between Friday and Sunday, since it gets better every time we heat it up and we want those three days to enjoy it. Gumbo is the reason for the big variety of hot sauces in my fridge. It's also one of the reasons I work out at least an hour every day. And it reminds me of when my family lived in Shreveport, Louisiana.

It's no accident that all of the food I'm passionate about leads back to family. It was Faith Ford, a born-and-raised Louisianan, though, who first introduced me to the food from the Creole State. She made an amazing gumbo, along with mind-blowing black-eyed peas that are a Southern tradition on New Year's Day. They're thought to bring good luck and wealth. But it wasn't until my youngest brother, Pat, married his wife, Stacy, who is also from Louisiana, that we all became gumbo zealots. You get a good sense of the two of them as soon as you find out their recipe begins with a six-pack of beer—and those are for the cooks (they assume at least two cooks) to consume as they make the gumbo. I've kept it to the basics here but if you'd like to see Pat and Stacy's recipe, go to my Web site ValerieBertinelli.com for a fun read.

I always say you can feed an army with their recipe. But you almost need an army to stand watch as you make it. They estimate it takes 2 to 5 hours, depending on the amount, the prep, and the number of beers. Tom and I spent forever the first time we made it. We had to take turns stirring the roux because our arms got so tired. The roux is a mix of flour and oil that you stir constantly so that it won't burn. If it burns, it's ruined, Stacy told us, and you have to start over. "But keep sipping your beer," she added.

After many years of practice, I have this step down to 20 minutes. The rest still takes time, and that's the point. Hurrying a gumbo would be about as pointless as mixing the rice into the same pot. It would ruin everything, including the time you spend sitting around visiting while the gumbo simmers. There's wisdom in all cooking.

After you've added your sausage and turkey (I don't like to mix sausage and shrimp), you only have one more crucial step. That's to taste it and decide if it's spicy enough for you. Pat and Stacy like in inhumanly hot. Tom is nearly as intemperate. You can find me a couple rungs down the heat ladder. What I like about this last step, though, is that it's like life itself. It's the Tao of gumbo. You decide how much fire you can handle—then go for it! Someone will usually rescue you with a cold drink if things get too hot. And that's a good life lesson, too.

Sides

Buy the very best quality vegetables you can find, then prepare them simply.

TOM AND I made artichokes last night. I wish you could have tasted them. They were perfectly ripe: heavy for their size, tight bright green leaves, with soft gold and purple insides bursting with an abundance of flesh. I have been making artichokes for decades, and luckily Tom also had them on his list of favorites when we met. But he liked them stuffed with bread crumbs and other goodies, the way his mother had made them, and I preferred them in their natural state.

Since then, I have converted Tom. Now we partially steam them, then season with salt, pepper, and olive oil, put them on the grill, and finish them off with a drizzle of thick balsamic syrup. That was our entire dinner last night. Mmmm.

I'm equally enthusiastic about vegetables in general. I probably wouldn't have admitted that in my twenties, but taste buds change, as did my knowledge about foods and what constituted a healthy diet. Now I am as pro-vegetable as is possible for one who still enjoys meat and fish. My affection began when I started Jenny Craig in 2007. In the first 6 months, I probably ate more fruits and vegetables than I had in the previous 10 years. I learned to roast them, grill them, steam them, and eat them raw.

They were free foods. I could have as many portions as I wanted, and I found I didn't need to have that many because they filled me up.

I also discovered they were full of all the vitamins, nutrients, and antioxidants that I was trying to consume with my multivitamins. So the bottles went in the trash, and instead I bought more broccoli—and spinach, snap peas, kale, carrots, and beets.

I forgot Brussels sprouts, and I shouldn't have. A member of the cabbage family and full of vitamins A and C and fiber, they're another maligned, misunderstood vegetable that has been a staple in my kitchen since I began cooking for myself at age 19. I'm not saying I ate them often back then, not like I do today. But they were always in my fridge. If a friend saw them on the counter, I'd always get asked, "How do you make these?" Well, I tell you my way in this chapter. But use that as a jumping-off point to find your own favorite. PS: They cook faster—and more evenly—if you slice them in half.

The best part of getting into vegetables is shopping for them. I don't mind stopping at the grocery store on my way home from the set. I'm also at my local farmers' market nearly every Sunday morning. Fresh makes a difference. The sight of them sitting on the counter, the greens spilling over the sides of my colander, just feels healthy. A good meal begins with your eyes, the anticipation growing from there. If there are veggies on the counter, I also know that Tom and I are going to spend some time together peeling and chopping, and that reminds me of when we first fell in love.

SAUTÉED SPINACH AND MUSHROOMS

A perfect side dish, this earthy mix is one of my favorites. When I crave greens, I turn to this easy sauté. And if there's any leftover, I fold it into a frittata the next morning.

YIELD
Serves 4

2 tablespoons extra-virgin olive oil

3 cloves garlic, smashed

2 cups sliced mushrooms

Kosher salt and freshly ground black pepper

10 ounces baby spinach

1–2 tablespoons balsamic vinegar

HEAT THE OIL in a medium sauté pan or skillet (not nonstick), over medium-low heat. Add the garlic and cook until fragrant, about 2 minutes (do not let the garlic brown). Push the garlic off to the side of the pan and add the mushrooms. Increase the heat to medium-high and season the mushrooms with salt and pepper to taste. Cook, stirring occasionally, until the mushrooms are cooked through and begin to become golden in spots, 10 to 12 minutes.

Add the spinach, sprinkle with an additional pinch of salt, and turn with tongs until wilted. (If you can't fit all the spinach in the pan, cover it for a few minutes, then uncover, stir, and add the rest.) Transfer to a serving platter, drizzle with the vinegar, and serve warm.

Per serving: *104 calories, 3 g protein, 11 g carbohydrates, 7 g total fat, 1 g saturated fat, 4 g fiber, 236 mg sodium*

PERFECT GRILLED ARTICHOKES

YIELD
Serves 4

1 lemon

4 large artichokes

3 tablespoons extra-virgin olive oil plus additional for rubbing over the steamed artichokes

1 tablespoon balsamic vinegar

1 clove garlic, pushed through a press

Kosher salt and freshly ground black pepper

Mint leaves

So beautiful. So healthy. Especially when you don't stuff them. My idea of a perfect leisurely lunch? An artichoke grilled to charred, buttery perfection and a glass of chilled sparkling wine.

PREPARE A LEMON bath by halving the lemon and squeezing the juice into a medium bowl. Drop the lemon halves in the bowl, too. Fill the bowl to within 2" of the rim with water.

Working with one artichoke at a time, cut off the stem so that it's flush with the bottom of the artichoke. Trim and peel the stem, halving lengthwise if it is thicker than one finger, and add to the bowl of lemon water. Peel away and discard the outer dark green leaves of the artichoke until only yellow-green leaves remain. Cut off the dark green tips of these leaves. Quarter the artichoke, and use a paring knife to remove and discard any pointy purplish leaves and the fuzzy choke at the heart of each artichoke. Place the quarters in the lemon water as you finish cleaning them. Repeat with the remaining artichokes.

Place the artichokes in a steamer basket inserted into a pan filled with 2" of boiling water. Cover and steam over high heat, until a paring knife inserted in the bottom of the choke comes out easily, 15 to 20 minutes.

Meanwhile, whisk together the 3 tablespoons oil, the vinegar, and garlic until emulsified. Set aside.

Lightly coat a grill rack with oil and preheat the grill on high for 5 minutes. Rub the artichoke quarters and stems lightly with some olive oil and season with salt and pepper. Reduce the heat to medium and place the artichokes over direct heat. Cook until grill marks appear, about 4 minutes. Arrange on a platter, drizzle with the vinaigrette and garnish with the mint. Serve warm.

Per serving: *189 calories, 6 g protein, 19 g carbohydrates, 13 g total fat, 2 g saturated fat, 9 g fiber, 213 mg sodium*

TOM'S GREEN BEANS WITH SHALLOTS

The best green beans I've ever had come from the farmers' market in Studio City, where I steer Tom toward the vegetables and away from the bacon-wrapped hot dogs. (I have yet to try one of those and can't imagine how long I'd have to work out to work one off!) This is our go-to vegetable dish. It goes with the Peppered Beef Tenderloin with Horseradish Sauce (page 149), Chicken Paillard with Salsa Verde (page 138), and Wolfie's Marinated Lamb Chops (page 155). Bring the beans to room temperature before serving.

YIELD

Serves 4

12 ounces green beans, topped and tailed

¼ cup extra-virgin olive oil

1 tablespoon sherry vinegar or red wine vinegar

1 teaspoon Dijon mustard

1 shallot, minced

Kosher salt and freshly ground black pepper

PLACE THE BEANS in a steamer basket set in a pot filled with 2" of boiling water. Cover and steam until the beans are bright green and still slightly firm to the bite, about 10 minutes.

Meanwhile, whisk together the oil, vinegar, mustard, shallot, and salt and pepper to taste. Pour the dressing over the beans and toss to coat. Cover and let marinate in the refrigerator overnight. Bring to room temperature and serve.

Per serving: *162 calories, 2 g protein, 10 g carbohydrates, 14 g total fat, 2 g saturated fat, 2 g fiber, 95 mg sodium*

ROASTED VEGETABLES WITH HERBS

Every vegetable has a friend in the herb garden. The fun starts when you experiment with the combinations that appeal to you. I am a huge fan of roasting just about every vegetable there is and have come up with a master recipe for cooking some of my favorites. The key is to cut the vegetables uniformly, in bite-size pieces.

Vegetables, cut into bite-size pieces or as instructed

Olive oil

Kosher salt and freshly ground black pepper

PREHEAT THE OVEN to 375°F. Toss the vegetables in enough olive oil to thoroughly coat. Season with salt and pepper. Spread the vegetables onto 2 large baking sheets, without crowding the sheets. Roast until browned around the edges and cooked through, about 35 minutes. Transfer to a platter or large bowl and serve.

Some Favorite Combinations

❀ Wedges of fennel and halved cherry tomatoes roasted, then tossed with chopped fresh fennel fronds or dill. Serve with Baked Side of Salmon with Honey Mustard Sauce (page 158).

❀ Cauliflower florets roasted, then tossed with rinsed capers and chopped fresh parsley. Serve with Peppered Beef Tenderloin with Horseradish Sauce (page 149).

❀ Broccoli rabe, halved cherry tomatoes, and halved shallots, roasted—check the broccoli rabe for doneness at 25 minutes. Serve with Peppered Beef Tenderloin with Horseradish Sauce (page 149).

❀ Asparagus, left whole, and garlic cloves in their skins, roasted and cooled. Squeeze the garlic out of their skins and mix with the asparagus. Drizzle with vincotto or balsamic vinegar, if desired. Serve with Baked Side of Salmon with Honey Mustard Sauce (page 158).

❀ Peeled sweet potatoes, cut into $1/2$" wedges, and new potatoes, scrubbed and halved or wedged if large, tossed with rosemary sprigs and roasted. Crumble the needles and toss. Serve with the Chicken Paillard with Salsa Verde (page 138).

❀ Eggplant, cubed or sliced into coins and roasted. Toss with chopped fresh basil or mint and a splash of balsamic vinegar. Serve with Wolfie's Marinated Lamb Chops (page 155).

❀ Baby beets, roasted, then tossed with chopped fresh tarragon and parsley. Serve with Wolfie's Marinated Lamb Chops (page 155) or for lunch, with Greens with Polenta Croutons (page 94).

In Praise of Cauliflower

I READ A REVIEW of an LA restaurant where the writer devoted a couple lines to the cauliflower side dish he had eaten and loved. After admitting he'd had a second helping, he asked his readers, when did cauliflower become hip? And when did it become addictively delicious? When I was growing up, cauliflower was always broccoli's pale, less-desirable cousin. It was an automatic "no thanks," and I'd pass the bowl to my brother. But now I find myself going into restaurants and looking down the menu for cauliflower before I even consider an entrée. These days, it's being prepared in so many ways: pureed, fried, au gratin with a little truffle oil, or, as I suggest here, roasted and tossed with capers and parsley or mashed like potatoes. I've put a medley of roasted vegetables in this chapter, and sometimes I make a whole meal out of them. And why not? As the aforementioned food critic discovered with cauliflower, they're addictively delicious.

Herbed Mashed Cauliflower

When I want to indulge in mashed potatoes but feel I should make a healthier choice, I prepare this delicious, creamy mash using whatever soft herbs I have on hand.

YIELD
Serves 4–6

BRING A MEDIUM pot of water to a boil. Add the cauliflower and let cook until fork-tender, about 8 minutes. Drain thoroughly and transfer to a food processor. Add the yogurt, butter, garlic, dill, and parsley and process until creamy. Season with salt and pepper to taste. Transfer to a warmed bowl, stir in the cheese and garnish with the dill and parsley. Serve hot.

Per serving (when serving 4): *91 calories, 8 g protein, 10 g carbohydrates, 3 g total fat, 2 g saturated fat, 3 g fiber, 175 mg sodium*

Per serving (when serving 6): *61 calories, 5 g protein, 7 g carbohydrates, 2 g total fat, 1 g saturated fat, 2 g fiber, 117 mg sodium*

1 head of cauliflower, cut into florets

1 container (6 ounces) 0% plain Greek yogurt

2 teaspoons butter

2 cloves garlic, minced

2 tablespoons chopped fresh dill plus additional for garnish

2 tablespoons chopped fresh flat-leaf parsley plus additional for garnish

Kosher salt and freshly ground pepper

2 tablespoons finely grated Parmigiano-Reggiano cheese

Brussels Sprouts with Pancetta

YIELD

Serves 6–8

2 pounds Brussels sprouts, any loose outer leaves trimmed and the sprouts halved, or quartered if large

2 tablespoons olive oil

1 ¼"-thick slice pancetta, cut into small cubes

2 cloves garlic, chopped

Kosher salt and white pepper

Cider vinegar (optional)

Brussels sprouts are the most underrated, overcooked vegetable I can think of. The trick is to buy very fresh ones, with tight bright leaves and no blemishes, and then cook them until they are easy to bite into but not mushy. Underdone sprouts, when the centers are still slightly raw, are a major turnoff, as they are when they're overcooked. I often eat these without the pancetta, but I never skip it when I make them for guests.

FILL A MEDIUM saucepan with several inches of salted water and bring to a boil. Add the sprouts and cook 2 to 3 minutes. Drain in a colander and rinse immediately under cold water. Drain well.

Heat the oil in a large sauté pan (not nonstick) over medium-low heat. Add the pancetta and sauté until browned in spots, about 8 minutes. Add the garlic and sauté until fragrant, about 3 minutes. Increase the heat to medium-high. Add the sprouts, spreading them out so that they are, for the most part, in a single layer. Season with salt and pepper. Cook, turning occasionally, until the sprouts are nicely golden in spots and are fork-tender, about 12 minutes. If the sprouts begin to brown all over and stick to the pan, add a splash of vinegar to the pan to help loosen the browned bits.

Transfer to a serving dish, add a splash of vinegar (if desired), and serve.

Per serving (when serving 6): *179 calories, 9 g protein, 14 g carbohydrates, 11 g total fat, 3 g saturated fat, 6 g fiber, 454 mg sodium*

Per serving (when serving 8): *134 calories, 7 g protein, 10 g carbohydrates, 9 g total fat, 2 g saturated fat, 4 g fiber, 341 mg sodium*

Acorn Squash with Baby Bitter Greens

I used to look forward to Thanksgiving for the acorn squash swimming in butter and maple syrup, but I've come up with a far healthier version that has now become a staple in my holiday repertoire. When it's cut into rings, seasoned with smoked paprika, and topped with crisp pumpkin seeds, the acorn squash flavor comes through as it should.

PREHEAT THE OVEN to 375°F. Scrub the acorn squash. Slice it crosswise into $\frac{1}{2}$" rings. Remove the pulp and seeds and discard. If the seeds are large, save them to roast with the pepitas.

Combine the squash rings with $\frac{1}{4}$ cup of the oil, a dash of the pimenton, and salt and pepper to taste in a large bowl and toss to coat. Toss the pepitas with a little oil, salt, pepper, and pimenton in a separate bowl. Spread the squash and pepitas on a large baking sheet, keeping the seeds in their own quadrant. Roast until the squash is tender and the seeds are crispy, 20 to 40 minutes, depending on how much moisture is in the pepitas.

Meanwhile, whisk together the vinegar, shallot, mustard, and sugar in a small bowl. Add the remaining $\frac{1}{4}$ cup oil in a steady stream, whisking constantly.

Toss the greens and cheese with half of the dressing in a large salad bowl. Season with salt and pepper and toss again. Arrange the squash rings over the top and drizzle with the remaining dressing. Scatter the pepitas over the squash and serve.

Per serving: *240 calories, 4 g protein, 8 g carbohydrates, 23 g total fat, 4 g saturated fat, 1 g fiber, 196 mg sodium*

YIELD
Serves 6

1 small acorn squash (about 1 pound)

$\frac{1}{2}$ cup extra-virgin olive oil plus additional for coating the pepitas

Pimenton (smoked paprika)

Kosher salt and freshly ground black pepper

2 tablespoons pepitas (hulled pumpkin seeds), toasted

1 tablespoon sherry vinegar

1 tablespoon minced shallot (from about $\frac{1}{2}$ small clove)

1 teaspoon grainy Dijon mustard

$\frac{1}{4}$ teaspoon sugar

4 ounces (8 cups) baby bitter greens, such as baby broccoli raab, arugula, mustard, and mizuna

2 ounces goat cheese, crumbled

STUFFED TOMATOES AND PEPPERS

YIELD

Serves 6

3 green bell peppers

3 beefsteak tomatoes

1 tablespoon extra-virgin olive oil plus additional for oiling the baking dish

½ onion, finely chopped

½ bulb fennel, cored, finely chopped, and fronds chopped

3 cloves garlic, minced

1 pound ground beef

1 teaspoon dried oregano

½ teaspoon ground cumin

¼ teaspoon ground cinnamon

1¼ teaspoons kosher salt plus additional for salting the vegetables

Freshly ground black pepper

2 cups cooked brown or white rice

1 cup loosely packed fresh flat-leaf parsley leaves, chopped

¼ cup panko bread crumbs

1 tablespoon unsalted butter, melted

2 large eggs, lightly beaten

This is one of Tom's mother's specialties, a quintessentially Italian dish. He likes to say that she would stuff any vegetable you put in front of her! Seasoned with oregano, cumin, and cinnamon, this super-comforting dish fills the house with gorgeous aromas.

BRING A LARGE pot of water to a boil. Meanwhile, trim away the tops of the bell peppers and tomatoes and scoop out the innards. Finely chop the tomato tops around the stems to make 1 cup and set aside. Discard the stems.

Cook the bell peppers in water for 3 minutes. Remove with a slotted spoon and rinse under cool water to stop the cooking. Set aside.

Preheat the oven to 350°F. Heat the oil in a medium skillet over medium-low heat. Add the onion and chopped fennel bulb and cook, stirring occasionally, until translucent, 8 minutes. Add 2 of the minced garlic cloves and cook until fragrant, about 1 minute.

Push the onions, fennel, and garlic to the edge of the skillet. Add the ground beef, oregano, cumin, cinnamon, 1 teaspoon of the salt and pepper to taste and increase the heat to medium-high. Cook the meat, breaking it up with the side of a wooden spoon, until browned all over and no longer pink. Add the reserved chopped tomatoes to the skillet and cook 3 minutes. Turn off the heat and add the rice, fennel fronds, and half of the parsley. Season to taste.

Combine the panko and the remaining parsley, garlic, and ¼ teaspoon salt in a small bowl. Pour the butter over and stir to combine.

Lightly salt and pepper the insides of the bell peppers and tomatoes. Stir the eggs into the meat mixture and divide it equally among the bell peppers and tomatoes. Top with the parsley-panko mixture, dividing it evenly among them.

Oil a baking dish just large enough to fit the bell peppers and tomatoes. Arrange them, alternating so that a tomato touches a pepper, which touches tomato, etc. Bake until the egg is thoroughly cooked and the rice is heated through, about 50 minutes. Let sit for 10 minutes before serving.

Per serving: *335 calories, 20 g protein, 26 g carbohydrates, 18 g total fat, 6 g saturated fat, 4 g fiber, 733 mg sodium*

LOVE APPLES?

TOM AND I ARE tomato freaks. We like them stuffed, cut into wedges and seasoned with a little salt and pepper, drizzled with balsamic vinegar, paired with burrata cheese, and chopped roughly and tossed into pasta. Talk about versatile. We only eat them in season, which is blissfully long in California, the perfect place to live for a tomato-mad couple like us. It seems I always have a bowl of them on my kitchen counter, which makes them easy to reach for when I want a snack. The funny thing is, it took me years to understand and appreciate tomatoes. On rainy days when I was little, my mother would make me a grilled cheese sandwich and a bowl of tomato soup, and that was my understanding of tomatoes for years—unless you count pasta sauce. I probably didn't see a fresh tomato until I moved to the West Coast! There's nothing quite like the variety available to us here; at the farmers' market, heirloom varieties are piled high in all of their colorful glory. The colors—from amber to apricot to persimmon—and curious shapes, are a feast for the eyes, which is where all great eating begins. There's almost nothing more satisfying than a perfectly ripe tomato sprinkled with a little salt. Eating well can be as simple as that.

MY VOICE

AS A LITTLE GIRL growing up in Delaware, I watched my mother cook. We lived in a modest split-level house on South Avon Drive, and the kitchen was her domain. She prepared three meals a day. It was the early 1960s, though, and our kitchen was isolated from the rest of the house by doors—not the center of the home like my kitchen is today—so I don't remember the sounds of her working in there.

Now, kitchens are open, and cooking is a social activity involving family and friends. It's considered modern, but it reminds me of the way my grandmother, my aunts, and my mother would cook together in my Aunt Adeline's basement kitchen. The look was different and the appliances were old, but it was inherently social—and loud—filled with nonstop conversation, laughter, the occasional crying child and the clatter of meal preparation.

So much of my cooking has been about re-creating those experiences, the comforting tastes and rich smells, and most importantly the sounds that came from my aunt's little kitchen. They were happy sounds. But I have also developed my own sounds—or what I call my own voice. Voice? If you're like me, voice is something you associate with writers and musicians, not chefs and certainly not women who prepare meals for family and friends.

However, even in the kitchen, we all have a distinct voice. If you were to ask my husband, Tom, or my son, Wolfie, they would tell you that my voice is extremely loud, that when I yell "dinner's ready," it echoes through the house like a seismic jolt. But I'm talking about the sounds we make in the kitchen, the music that results as we prepare the food: the chopping of vegetables, the sizzle of oil and garlic in a pan, the clank of oven racks being rearranged, and the ring of a timer.

My voice emerged after I started Jenny Craig in 2007 and woke up to the foods I was putting into my body. Until then, my voice in the kitchen had been mostly silent. I made meals, but I didn't celebrate them. Although I made sure my son ate well, I myself consumed frozen foods that didn't require much preparation beyond a baking sheet. I snuck in and out of the kitchen at night.

All that changed when I changed my diet. As I lost weight, I found a new attitude and approach. The foods I ate got fresher and needed peeling and chopping. I spent more time preparing dishes than actually eating. Tom came into my life and we played music in the kitchen as we cooked and talked. I was happier with myself. The kitchen turned into the heartbeat of our home. Wolfie and Tom's children hung out. The noise level increased, but it was a good, hearty, healthy, and happy noise, the sound of family and life.

It was like my Aunt Adeline's, but different. It was mine. This is my voice—and why I love to cook.

Cooking with my mother and brother in our Shreveport, Louisiana, kitchen

Desserts

Dessert is not a dirty word in
my house. Moderation is the key.

L IFE IS FULL of pleasures, whether it's a European vacation, a 2-hour massage, or a new pair of shoes. They are treats. And so it is with dessert. I suppose I am lucky. My everyday cravings tend more toward savory than sweet. But then, all of a sudden, my body will change channels on me and I want dessert. I eat it, too. Dessert is not a dirty word in my house—not as dirty as me asking, "Honey, what do you think of these new shoes?" I don't have dessert often, and when I do, I keep the portions small or limit myself to one or two cookies. Moderation is the key, as is being realistic. If it's my birthday or a special occasion, I know that I am going to celebrate, and I enjoy myself without guilt. I plan accordingly. I don't go crazy. And I don't make myself crazy, either. If I'm going to splurge, I call it a splurge. I don't call it a cheat day, and neither should you. All you're doing is messing with your mind.

I love citrus in my desserts. That natural zing on my palate does it for me. I have included a few desserts here for those of you who feel the same way. Key Lime Pie (page 206) and Lemon Meringue Pie (page 208) are favorites, and a thin slice of either one provides me with a delicious finish to a special meal. Honestly, at this point in my life, I don't even consider those a splurge. I am working out and eating properly, so why not?

The other desserts in this section range from the Panna Cotta with Frutti di Bosco (page 213), which Wolfie always requests when he comes home after a stint on the road, to the Neapolitan Cookies (page 219) and Russian Tea Cakes (page 225) that my mother made for the holidays. Every year at Christmastime, she turned into a one-woman cookie factory, filling tins lined with parchment paper and sending them to friends and relatives as gifts. Just thinking about her Pizzelles (page 216) as I type this sentence makes my mouth water.

Unfortunately, her wonderful tradition ended with me; I don't spend the holiday baking. On the other hand, I make these cookies more than once a year. The Pecan Pie (page 211) recipe dates back to when I began living on my own in my late teens and early twenties, back when I didn't worry that a single slice has more than 500 calories. Now, it's a rare treat, and to be honest, I get as much enjoyment from watching other people savor a heavenly slice as I do eating it myself. Likewise with Lynn's Sick Brownie Bites (page 201), which earned their name from years of people taking a bite of my friend's treats and saying the same thing: "That's sick!" Those delightful reactions are better than dessert—and they don't have any calories at all.

BLUEBERRY TART

A cakey crust is pressed into the pan (no rolling out the dough!), then filled with spiced fresh blueberries. It's as easy as that. Last time I made it for the kids it disappeared faster than they could say, "More, please!" If you're lucky enough to have leftovers, it's great in the morning, cold, with a hot cup of joe.

YIELD
Serves 8

Cooking spray

1 cup plus 1 tablespoon all-purpose flour

$\frac{1}{3}$ cup plus $1\frac{1}{2}$ tablespoons granulated sugar

$\frac{1}{4}$ teaspoon kosher salt

$\frac{1}{2}$ cup (1 stick) unsalted butter, cut into pieces

2 egg yolks

4 cups blueberries

Grated zest of 1 lemon

1 tablespoon freshly squeezed lemon juice

$\frac{1}{2}$ teaspoon ground cinnamon

$\frac{1}{4}$ teaspoon nutmeg

Confectioners' sugar for dusting

PREHEAT THE OVEN to 375°F. Coat a 9" springform pan with cooking spray.

Combine 1 cup of the flour, $1\frac{1}{2}$ tablespoons of the granulated sugar, and the salt in a food processor and pulse to combine. Add the butter and pulse until the mixture resembles coarse meal with some large lumps. Add the egg yolks and pulse until blended.

Place the dough in the springform pan, and press evenly against the bottom and about 1" up the sides.

Toss $2\frac{1}{2}$ cups of the berries, the lemon zest, juice, cinnamon, nutmeg, remaining 1 tablespoon flour, and remaining $\frac{1}{3}$ cup granulated sugar in a medium bowl. Pour the berry mixture into the shell. Bake until vigorously bubbling, about 1 hour. Remove from the oven and immediately top with the remaining $1\frac{1}{2}$ cups blueberries. Just before serving, dust with confectioners' sugar by tapping it through a fine-mesh sieve. Serve warm or at room temperature.

Per serving: *262 calories, 3 g protein, 35 g carbohydrates, 13 g total fat, 8 g saturated fat, 3 g fiber, 78 mg sodium*

Chocolate-Ginger Mousse Cones

YIELD

Makes 30/Serves 15

MOUSSE

8 ounces bittersweet chocolate

3 cups chilled heavy cream

CONES

1⅓ cups all-purpose flour

⅔ cup sugar

3 tablespoons ground ginger

2 teaspoons baking powder

¼ teaspoon ground cinnamon

⅛ teaspoon ground cloves

Pinch kosher salt

½ cup (1 stick) unsalted butter, melted and cooled slightly

½ cup whole milk

2 large eggs

1 teaspoon vanilla extract

Cooking spray

A variation on a Jenny Craig recipe, these delectable little treats may seem indulgent, but they're just large enough to satisfy and not so large that you feel guilty after eating one. Make them with a partner—one of you bakes and shapes the pizzelle cones, while the other fills them with the creamy mousse. A pizzelle maker, which comes with the small wooden cone mold, is essential. Fill the cones with the mousse just before serving; they'll become soggy if filled too far in advance.

TO MAKE THE MOUSSE: Place a medium bowl in the freezer for 10 minutes. Meanwhile, melt the chocolate in a medium microwaveable bowl on low power, about 3 minutes. Let cool slightly. Pour the cream into the chilled bowl and whip until it holds stiff peaks. Fold one-third of the cream into the chocolate. Fold half of the remaining cream into the chocolate and then the remaining cream. Refrigerate until ready to use.

TO MAKE THE CONES: Preheat a pizzelle iron. Whisk together the flour, sugar, ginger, baking powder, cinnamon, cloves, salt, butter, milk, eggs, and vanilla extract until smooth. Coat the pizzelle iron with the cooking spray, then close to continue heating.

When the iron is hot, spoon about 1 tablespoon of the batter onto each side. Slowly close and let cook until golden, 50 seconds to 1 minute. Immediately roll one of the cookies around the wooden cone mold, slide it off, and transfer to a rack to cool completely. Leave the other cookie on the iron while you work with the first one—it will firm up if you take it off the heat. Continue cooking and rolling in this way with the remaining batter.

Just before serving, fill a large resealable plastic bag with the mousse and snip one corner. Dividing evenly, pipe the mousse into the cones. Serve immediately.

Per serving: *395 calories, 4 g protein, 28 g carbohydrates, 32 g total fat, 19 g saturated fat, 2 g fiber, 92 mg sodium*

SICILIAN LOVE CAKE

YIELD

Serves 12

Canola oil for preparing the pan

BATTER

3 cups all-purpose flour

2 cups sugar

1/2 cup unsweetened cocoa powder

2 teaspoons baking soda

1/2 teaspoon kosher salt

2 tablespoons distilled white
   vinegar

1 teaspoon vanilla extract

MASCARPONE-RICOTTA FILLING

1/2 cup plus 2 tablespoons
   (5 ounces) mascarpone

1/2 cup (4 ounces) ricotta cheese

1 large egg

1/3 cup sugar

1/8 teaspoon kosher salt

COCOA-MASCARPONE FROSTING

1 1/4 cups (10 ounces) mascarpone

1 tablespoon unsweetened cocoa
   powder

1 tablespoon sugar

1 tablespoon whole milk

Tom's dad sends us *La Gazzetta Italiana*, an Italian newspaper that he loves the way we do the *Los Angeles Times*. I always go straight to the food page, where I was reminded of this sheet cake, which is not your average after-school-snacking cake. Dollops of mascarpone mixed with ricotta are baked into the chocolate batter, and the whole thing is frosted with cocoa-infused mascarpone. Now that's love.

PREHEAT THE OVEN to 350°F. Coat a 9" x 13" baking dish with oil.

TO MAKE THE BATTER: Combine the flour, sugar, cocoa, baking soda, and salt in a medium bowl and whisk until thoroughly incorporated. Stir in the vinegar, vanilla extract, and 2 cups water. Pour the batter into the prepared dish and set aside.

TO MAKE THE FILLING: Combine the mascarpone, ricotta, egg, sugar, and salt in a small bowl and whisk until smooth. Drop the filling in 8 equal portions onto the cake batter. Bake until a skewer inserted in the center comes out clean, about 40 minutes.

TO MAKE THE FROSTING: Just before serving, whisk together the mascarpone, cocoa, sugar, and milk in a small bowl until smooth. Using an offset spatula, spread the frosting evenly all over the cake and serve.

Per serving: *513 calories, 9 g protein, 67 g carbohydrates, 25 g total fat, 13 g saturated fat, 2 g fiber, 375 mg sodium*

Italian Sponge Cake

YIELD

Serves 10–12

CAKE

Cooking spray

1½ cups cake flour plus additional for flouring the pans

8 large eggs, separated

2¾ cups confectioners' sugar

1½ teaspoons vanilla extract

1 tablespoons baking powder

¾ teaspoon kosher salt

CREAM FILLING

¼ cup cornstarch

4 cups whole milk

2 teaspoons vanilla extract

¼ cup granulated sugar

⅛ teaspoon kosher salt

Grated zest of 1 lemon

3 egg yolks

ICING

1½ cups chilled heavy cream

2 tablespoons granulated sugar

Every Italian Nonnie knows how to make a good sponge cake, mine included. She passed it on to my mom, who passed it on to me. And so it goes. It's the kind of cake that's wide open to variation in the filling. A sweet cream filling is traditional, but my mom spikes the chocolate pudding with a little rum and spreads it between layers. A good blood orange jam or lemon or lime curd works, too.

PREHEAT THE OVEN to 350°F. Coat two 10" cake pans with cooking spray, and flour the bottoms and sides generously, tapping out the excess.

TO MAKE THE CAKE: In the bowl of an electric mixer fitted with the whisk attachment, beat the egg whites until stiff peaks form. Transfer to a clean bowl and set aside.

Clean the bowl and whisk attachment of the mixer and beat the egg yolks until pale yellow and creamy. Add the confectioners' sugar and vanilla extract and beat until thoroughly incorporated. Whisk together the 1½ cups flour, the baking powder, and salt in a small bowl. Fold one-third of the egg whites into the egg yolk batter, then half of the flour mixture. Repeat with half of the remaining egg whites, the remaining flour mixture, then the rest of the egg whites.

Pour the batter into the prepared pans and bake until a skewer inserted in the center comes out clean, about 25 minutes. Transfer to a rack to cool, about 15 minutes. Turn the cakes out of the pans onto the racks to cool completely.

TO MAKE THE FILLING: Whisk together the cornstarch and 1 cup of the milk in a small bowl. Set aside.

Combine the vanilla extract, granulated sugar, salt, lemon zest, and the remaining 3 cups milk in a large saucepan and warm over medium heat. Give the cornstarch mixture a good whisk and slowly add it to the warm milk mixture, whisking constantly. Bring the mixture to a boil, then reduce the heat and simmer, whisking constantly, about 3 minutes. Remove the pan from the heat.

Lightly beat the egg yolks in a medium bowl. Whisk about $\frac{1}{2}$ cup of the hot milk mixture into the egg yolks, then pour the yolks back into the saucepan, whisking constantly. Return the saucepan to the heat, bring back to a simmer, and cook for 3 minutes. Pour the mixture into a medium heatproof bowl and cover with plastic wrap, pressing the wrap directly against the surface of the mixture. Refrigerate until thoroughly chilled, about 2 hours.

TO MAKE THE ICING: While chilling the filling, combine the heavy cream and sugar in the bowl of an electric mixture fitted with the whisk attachment. Beat until sturdy peaks form. Cover and refrigerate until ready to assemble the cake.

To assemble the cake, use a serrated knife to slice each cake layer in half horizontally to make four layers. Reserve the bottom half of one of the cake layers for the top layer of the cake. Place one of the remaining layers on a cake plate and spread one-third of the filling onto the top. Top with a second cake layer. Spread half of the remaining filling on top of it. Arrange a third cake layer over it and spread the top with the remaining filling. Set the reserved layer on top so that the smooth bottom side is the top of the cake. Spread the icing all over the top and sides of the cake. Serve immediately.

Per serving (when serving 10): *510 calories, 11 g protein, 67 g carbohydrates, 22 g total fat, 12 g saturated fat, 1 g fiber, 428 mg sodium*

Per serving (when serving 12): *425 calories, 10 g protein, 56 g carbohydrates, 18g total fat, 10 g saturated fat, 0 g fiber, 357 mg sodium*

Mrs. Van Halen's Spekkoek

Mrs. Van Halen used to make this many-, many-, many-layered Dutch-Indonesian cake on a whim the way you and I might make a snack cake. It's not for the faint of heart—I remember it taking her all morning to bake—but the results are so delish and impressive, it's worth putting in the time. Be sure to use a fresh round of wax paper when baking the final layer, to ensure a neat release for the top layer of the cake.

YIELD

Serves 8–12

Cooking spray

1 cup (2 sticks) unsalted butter, softened, plus 10 tablespoons melted

$\frac{3}{4}$ cup plus $1\frac{1}{2}$ teaspoons granulated sugar

$2\frac{1}{2}$ teaspoons ground cinnamon

1 cup all-purpose flour

5 large eggs, separated

1 teaspoon vanilla extract

$\frac{1}{8}$ teaspoon kosher salt

$1\frac{1}{2}$ teaspoons ground cardamom

1 teaspoon ground anise

1 teaspoon ground cloves

1 teaspoon ground nutmeg

Confectioners' sugar for dusting

PREHEAT THE OVEN to 400°F. Coat the bottoms and sides of three 8" cake pans with the cooking spray. Line the bottom of each with a round of wax or parchment paper. Coat the paper with more spray.

Combine the melted butter, $1\frac{1}{2}$ teaspoons of the granulated sugar, and $\frac{3}{4}$ teaspoon of the cinnamon in a bowl and stir to combine. Set aside and have a pastry brush ready.

In the bowl of an electric mixer, beat together the softened butter and the remaining $\frac{3}{4}$ cup granulated sugar on medium-high until light and fluffy, about 7 minutes. Reduce the speed to low and add the flour, egg yolks, vanilla extract, and salt in several additions, and beat until just combined.

In a separate bowl and using clean beaters, beat the egg whites on high speed until they hold stiff peaks. Using a rubber spatula, gently fold the whites into the cake batter in thirds until well combined. Divide the batter evenly between 2 bowls. Whisk together the cardamom, anise, cloves, nutmeg, and remaining $1\frac{3}{4}$ teaspoons cinnamon. Using a rubber spatula, fold the spice mixture into one of the bowls of batter.

Spread a very thin layer of the plain batter into two of the prepared pans, about 2 heaping tablespoons each, and use the back of a soup spoon to spread it all the way out to the sides. Do not worry if there are some transparent spots in the interior. Spread a very thin layer of the spiced batter, about 2 heaping tablespoons, into the third pan, and spread as above. Bake until just set, about 5 minutes. Let cool for 1 minute.

(continued)

Working with one cake layer at a time and beginning with a plain layer, run a small offset spatula around the edge, slide the spatula underneath the wax paper, and turn the layer out onto a cake plate. Peel off the wax paper and return it to the pan. Lightly brush the layer with the cinnamon butter mixture. Turn the spiced layer out onto the first layer and brush with the cinnamon butter mixture. Repeat with the remaining plain layer and brush with the cinnamon butter mixture.

Return the wax paper rounds to their respective pans and coat again with cooking spray. Spread the spiced batter as above into two pans and the plain batter into the third pan. Bake, layer, and brush with the cinnamon butter mixture as above. Continue baking, layering, and brushing the layers in this manner, alternating the batters with each layer. For the top layer, replace the wax paper with a new sheet and coat with cooking spray so that the visible surface will be smooth.

Dust the top of the cake generously with the confectioners' sugar and serve warm.

Per serving (when serving 8): *525 calories, 6 g protein, 34 g carbohydrates, 42 g total fat, 16 g saturated fat, 1 g fiber, 87 mg sodium*

Per serving (when serving 12): *350 calories, 4 g protein, 22 g carbohydrates, 28 g total fat, 17 g saturated fat, 1 g fiber, 58 mg sodium*

Classic Gooey Brownies

YIELD

Makes 16

BROWNIES

Cooking spray

¾ cup (1½ sticks) unsalted butter

4 ounces unsweetened chocolate

3 large eggs, at room temperature

1½ cups granulated sugar

1 teaspoon instant espresso powder

1 teaspoon vanilla extract

1 cup all-purpose flour

1 teaspoon kosher salt

1½ cups dark chocolate chips

ICING

2 tablespoons low-fat buttermilk

1 tablespoon brewed coffee

½ cup confectioners' sugar

3 tablespoons unsweetened cocoa powder

What more can I say? These brownies are exactly as their name suggests. Incredibly gooey, oozing with chocolate, and impossible to cut into perfect squares. They may not be pretty, but no one will notice after that first bite.

TO MAKE THE BROWNIES: Preheat the oven to 375°F. Line an 8" x 8" square baking pan with parchment paper so that the paper overhangs two sides of the pan. Coat the parchment and sides of the pan with cooking spray.

Combine the butter and chocolate in the top of a double boiler and melt over medium heat. Set aside to cool slightly. Whisk the eggs in a large bowl until pale yellow. Add the granulated sugar, espresso powder, and vanilla extract to the eggs and whisk until fluffy. Whisk together the flour and salt in a small bowl.

Pour the chocolate mixture over the egg mixture and whisk until smooth. Fold in the flour mixture until just combined. Stir in the chocolate chips. Transfer the batter to the pan, spreading it to the edges with an offset spatula or the back of a spoon. Bake until the batter is set and cracked on top, about 30 minutes. Remove and let cool on a rack.

TO MAKE THE ICING: Whisk together the buttermilk, coffee, confectioners' sugar, and cocoa powder until smooth.

Remove the cooled brownies from the pan by using the parchment overhang to lift them out. Pour the icing over the top and spread with a small offset spatula. Let dry. Cut into squares and serve.

Per serving: 226 calories, 3 g protein, 27 g carbohydrates, 14 g total fat, 8 g saturated fat, 2 g fiber, 105 mg sodium

LYNN'S SICK BROWNIE BITES

I have my friend Lynn to thank for these chocolatey nuggets. Studded with coconut and walnuts, they are as indulgent as it gets.

YIELD
Makes 18–20

PREHEAT THE OVEN to 375°F. Coat an 8" x 8" baking pan with cooking spray.

Combine the graham crackers, chocolate chips, condensed milk, coconut, walnuts, and salt in a medium bowl. Stir with a wooden spoon until thoroughly combined. Transfer the mixture to the prepared pan and press to the edges. Bake until the chocolate melts and the top is golden, 15 to 20 minutes. Stir the hot mixture in the pan until the chocolate is incorporated throughout. Press back out to the edges and set aside until cool enough to handle.

Spread the confectioners' sugar on a dinner plate. Scoop out the brownie mixture by the tablespoon and shape into balls. While still warm, roll each ball in the sugar to coat. The bonbons will keep, tightly covered, for 2 days.

Cooking spray

1²⁄₃ cups graham cracker crumbs

6 ounces semisweet chocolate chips

1 can (14 ounces) sweetened condensed milk

²⁄₃ cup shredded coconut

²⁄₃ cup chopped walnuts

¼ teaspoon kosher salt

Confectioners' sugar

Per cookie (when serving 18): *198 calories, 3 g protein, 37 g carbohydrates, 10 g total fat, 4 g saturated fat, 1 g fiber, 118 mg sodium*

Per cookie (when serving 20): *178 calories, 3 g protein, 24 g carbohydrates, 9 g total fat, 4 g saturated fat, 1 g fiber, 106 mg sodium*

SALTED HAZELNUT TOFFEE

YIELD

Makes about 5 cups /
Serves 20 (¼ cup per serving)

2 cups hazelnuts

Cooking spray

1 cup (2 sticks) unsalted butter

1 cup sugar

⅛ teaspoon kosher salt

1 cup dark chocolate chips

Coarse sea salt for sprinkling

This recipe is inspired by Tom's friend Lauri Stephenson, who presented me with a big, beautiful jar of homemade almond toffee as a thank you for hiring her husband to do some work at our home. I returned the empty jar to Lauri, who insisted it was part of the gift. I begged her to take it—and fill it back up with this completely addictive treat! Instead of begging Lauri a third time, and because I love hazelnuts so much, I came up with this version. Thank you, Lauri! A candy thermometer is key; without one, it's a challenge to cook the sugar properly.

PREHEAT THE OVEN to 350°F. Line a baking sheet with a nonstick silicone liner. Roast the hazelnuts until fragrant, about 10 minutes. Remove them to a plate and coat the liner with cooking spray.

Combine the butter, sugar, and salt in a medium saucepan and bring to a boil, whisking until the sugar and butter are melted. Cook, whisking occasionally, until the mixture registers 300°F on a candy thermometer. Watch the thermometer closely because the last 40°F of cooking go very fast. Immediately remove from the heat and stir in the hazelnuts.

Pour the mixture onto the baking sheet and smooth with an offset spatula. Let dry for about 1½ minutes, then scatter chocolate chips on top. As they melt, spread the chocolate to the outer edges of the toffee with an offset spatula. Sprinkle with sea salt and freeze until set, about 30 minutes. Peel the toffee away from the silicone liner and transfer to a cutting board. Cut into pieces with a sharp knife. The toffee will keep, tightly covered, up to 1 week.

Per serving: *260 calories, 3 g protein, 18 g carbohydrates, 22 g total fat, 9 g saturated fat, 2 g fiber, 95 mg sodium*

ROBIN'S FRUIT "PIZZA"

My sister-in-law Robin is the genius behind this spectacularly simple dessert: essentially shortcake dough rolled out like a pizza and topped with mascarpone and fresh berries. Perfectly ripe peaches, cut into thin wedges, would make a nice topping, too.

YIELD
Serves 8–12

2 cups all-purpose flour plus additional for dusting the work surface

1 tablespoon baking powder

½ teaspoon kosher salt

3 tablespoons plus 1 teaspoon sugar

1 cup light cream

3 tablespoons salted butter, melted

3 cups mixed berries, such as strawberries, blackberries, blueberries, and raspberries

1 teaspoon vanilla extract

¼ cup fresh mint leaves, cut into thin strips, plus a few whole leaves for garnish

8 ounces mascarpone

PREHEAT THE OVEN to 450°F. Line 2 baking sheets with parchment paper or nonstick silicone liners.

Combine the flour, baking powder, salt, and 2 tablespoons of the sugar in a large bowl. Using a rubber spatula, stir in the cream and butter until the dough comes together. Knead several times in the bowl, then divide into 2 balls.

Lightly flour a rolling pin and a clean work surface. Roll out each dough ball into an 8" round. Transfer the rounds to the baking sheets and bake until golden, about 15 minutes. Let cool.

Meanwhile, combine the berries with 1 teaspoon of the sugar, the vanilla extract, and mint in a large bowl. Let sit at room temperature.

Combine the mascarpone with the remaining 1 tablespoon sugar and whisk until light and fluffy.

Assemble the "pizza" just before serving. Spread half of the sweetened mascarpone over each shortcake. Top each with half of the berries and garnish with the mint leaves. Cut into wedges and serve.

Per serving (when serving 8): *381 calories, 7 g protein, 37 g carbohydrates, 24 g total fat, 13 g saturated fat, 3 g fiber, 341 mg sodium*

Per serving (when serving 12): *254 calories, 4 g protein, 25 g carbohydrates, 16 g total fat, 9 g saturated fat, 2 g fiber, 227 mg sodium*

CHERRY CLAFOUTI

YIELD

Serves 8

Butter for the baking dish

4 large eggs, separated

$2/3$ cup sugar

6 tablespoons all-purpose flour

1 cup heavy cream

2 teaspoons vanilla extract

$1/2$ teaspoon kosher salt

$1\frac{1}{2}$ pounds black or white cherries, pitted, or $1\frac{1}{4}$ pounds frozen pitted cherries, thawed and drained

Heaping $1/2$ teaspoon grated lemon zest

Whipped cream for topping

I make this at least a half dozen times every summer, when the cherries are loaded with juice. I love lemon zest and invariably add more than is called for in any recipe containing it; the same is true here. Use as much or as little as you please.

PREHEAT THE OVEN to 375°F. Butter a 12" oval or round baking dish.

Combine the egg yolks and $1/3$ cup of the sugar in a large bowl. Using a handheld mixer, beat on medium-high speed until ribbons form when you lift the beater just slightly out of the batter, about 8 minutes. Add the flour, heavy cream, and vanilla extract. Reduce the speed to low and beat until thoroughly blended, stopping the mixer occasionally to scrape down the sides of the bowl with a rubber spatula.

Slide the prepared baking dish into the oven to preheat for 4 to 5 minutes. Meanwhile, whisk together the egg whites and salt in a small bowl for about 30 seconds. Add to the batter and beat with the mixer on low speed until just incorporated, 1 to 2 minutes.

Combine the cherries, lemon zest, and the remaining $1/3$ cup sugar in a medium bowl, and stir until the cherries are thoroughly coated. Remove the pan from the oven, pour in the cherries, and top with the batter. Bake until set in the middle, 30 to 35 minutes. Serve warm with a small dollop of whipped cream.

Per serving: *287 calories, 5 g protein, 36 g carbohydrates, 14 g total fat, 8 g saturated fat, 2 g fiber, 196 mg sodium*

The Family That Cooks Together . . .

CLAFOUTI IS ONE OF the easiest desserts in my repertoire. It's also a crowd-pleaser that played an important role in our family. It was summer, and my relationship with Tom had turned serious, but his kids were a little slower to come around. One day, I was paging through a catalog from a cookware store and saw a recipe for this French dessert next to a picture of the baking dish they suggested making it in. I bought the dish, made the dessert, and the kids loved it. They clamored for more, and better yet, they asked if they could help make it. Some wanted to pit the cherries, some wanted to prep the batter, another wanted to pour it into the dish. All of them chimed in when it was ready: "Valerie, the timer went off!" I made it at least a half dozen times that summer. It brought everyone together and helped blend the family. Needless to say, I've been making it ever since.

KEY LIME PIE

I learned to make this out of pure love for it. For the longest time, I felt I should leave this one to the pastry chefs, but the truth is, it's as easy as cooking the filling and pouring it into a prepared graham cracker crust. You can make this with bottled Key lime juice, but it doesn't get any better than squeezing it from fresh Key limes.

YIELD

Makes 1 (8½") pie / Serves 6–8

Grated zest of 1 Key lime plus thinly sliced rounds for garnish

1¼ cups Key lime juice (26 to 32 Key limes)

1 can (14 ounces) sweetened condensed milk

1 cup whole milk

1 large egg

3 tablespoons cornstarch

1 prepared 8½" graham cracker crust

WHISK TOGETHER THE lime zest, juice, condensed milk, whole milk, egg, and cornstarch in a large saucepan. Bring to a boil over high heat, whisking constantly, then reduce the heat and simmer 2 minutes.

Pour the filling into the crust and let cool slightly, about 10 minutes. Cover with plastic wrap and place in the freezer until set, about 4 hours. Arrange the Key lime slices on top for garnish. Serve chilled. The pie can be stored, covered in the refrigerator, until ready to serve.

Per serving (when serving 6): *474 calories, 9 g protein, 72 g carbohydrates, 18 g total fat, 7 g saturated fat, 1 g fiber, 342 mg sodium*

Per serving (when serving 8): *356 calories, 7 g protein, 54 g carbohydrates, 13 g total fat, 5 g saturated fat, 1 g fiber, 257 mg sodium*

PUMPKIN PIE

I've been making pumpkin pie ever since I left home to live on my own. It's always on my Thanksgiving table, but I tend to make it throughout the fall and winter, when cinnamon, nutmeg, ginger, and cloves are the spices I crave. I have a heavy hand when it comes to seasoning the pumpkin filling, so taste it and season according to your own preferences. The pie dough recipe makes enough for two single-crust pies; wrap the excess in two layers of plastic wrap, put in a resealable plastic bag, and freeze for another time.

YIELD
Makes 1 (8") pie/Serves 6–8

Flour for dusting the work surface

½ recipe Mom's Flaky Pie Dough (page 210)

1¾ cups canned solid-pack pumpkin puree

1¼ cups light cream

⅓ cup plus 2 tablespoons firmly packed light brown sugar

2½ teaspoons ground cinnamon

1½ teaspoons nutmeg

1 teaspoon ground ginger

½ teaspoon ground cloves

¼ teaspoon kosher salt

2 large eggs, lightly beaten

2 teaspoons vanilla extract

2 tablespoons bourbon

Whipped cream for serving (optional)

ON A WELL-FLOURED surface and with a well-floured rolling pin, roll the dough into a 9" to 10" round. If the rolling pin and work surface quickly become sticky, refrigerate the dough until firm or, using a large spatula or bench scraper, transfer the dough to an 8" pie plate and press it into shape. Crimp the edges and prick the bottom all over with a fork. Refrigerate the pie shell for 20 minutes.

Meanwhile, preheat the oven to 325°F. Place a sheet of parchment paper or foil in the pie shell and fill with pie weights, raw rice, or dried beans. Bake until the edges are lightly golden, about 15 minutes. Remove the weights and paper, and bake until golden and cooked on the bottom and sides, 15 minutes more. Reduce the oven to 300°F.

Combine the pumpkin, cream, brown sugar, cinnamon, nutmeg, ginger, cloves, and salt in a large bowl and whisk until thoroughly blended. Stir in the eggs, vanilla, and bourbon. Whisk again until thoroughly blended.

Pour the pumpkin mixture into the pie shell and smooth the top with an offset spatula. Bake until the center wobbles slightly when shaken, 1 hour to 1 hour 10 minutes. Cool completely on a rack for about 2 hours. Serve with whipped cream, if desired.

Per serving (when serving 6): *423 calories, 7 g protein, 45 g carbohydrates, 24 g total fat, 14 g saturated fat, 3 g fiber, 346 mg sodium*

Per serving (when serving 8): *317 calories, 5 g protein, 34 g carbohydrates, 18 g total fat, 11 g saturated fat, 3 g fiber, 259 mg sodium*

LEMON MERINGUE PIE

YIELD

Makes 1 (8") pie / Serves 6–8

PIE DOUGH AND FILLING

Flour for dusting the work surface

½ recipe Mom's Flaky Pie Dough (page 210)

⅓ cup cornstarch

½ cup whole milk

5 large egg yolks

1 cup sugar

¼ teaspoon kosher salt

Grated zest of 1 lemon

¾ cup freshly squeezed lemon juice (from about 4 lemons)

2 tablespoons unsalted butter, cut up

MERINGUE

6 large egg whites, at room temperature

½ teaspoon cream of tartar

¾ cup sugar

⅛ teaspoon kosher salt

If there was a homemade lemon meringue pie in the house, it meant that something very special was going on. My mother only made this occasionally, and when she did, it didn't last very long. You're only going to need enough pie dough for a single crust, so wrap the excess in two layers of plastic wrap, put in a resealable plastic bag, and freeze for another time.

TO MAKE THE PIE DOUGH AND FILLING: Have ready an 8" pie plate. On a well-floured surface and using a generously floured rolling pin, roll the dough into a 9" to 10" round and transfer to the pie plate. If the rolling pin and work surface quickly become sticky, refrigerate the dough until firm or, using a large spatula or bench scraper, transfer the dough to the pie plate and press it into shape. Crimp the edges and prick the bottom all over with a fork. Refrigerate the pie shell for 20 minutes.

Meanwhile, preheat the oven to 350°F. Place a sheet of parchment paper or foil in the pie shell and fill with pie weights, raw rice, or dried beans. Bake until the edges are lightly golden, about 15 minutes. Remove the weights and paper, and bake until golden and cooked on the bottom and sides, 15 minutes more. Keep the oven on.

Whisk together the cornstarch and milk in a small bowl. Whisk together the egg yolks, sugar, salt, and 1 cup water in a heavy medium saucepan. Add the cornstarch mixture, lemon zest, and juice and whisk until thoroughly incorporated. Bring to a boil over medium heat, whisking, then reduce the heat. Simmer until very thick, 1 to 2 minutes. Remove from the heat and whisk in the butter until incorporated. Cover the mixture with plastic wrap or wax paper pressed right against its surface and set aside.

TO MAKE THE MERINGUE: Combine the egg whites, cream of tartar, sugar, and salt in the bowl of an electric mixer fitted with the whisk attachment. Beat on medium speed until the whites hold stiff peaks.

(continued)

Pour the warm filling into the pie shell and smooth the top with an offset spatula. Spread the meringue over the filling to cover it completely. Bake until the meringue browns in spots, 15 to 20 minutes. Cool completely on a rack about 3 hours. Serve at room temperature.

Mom's Flaky Pie Dough

▶ YIELD
Makes enough for 1 (8") double-crust pie or 2 (8") single-crust pies

2¼ cups all-purpose flour

1 tablespoon sugar

1 teaspoon kosher salt

¾ cup (1½ sticks) unsalted butter, cut up

6–8 tablespoons ice water

COMBINE THE FLOUR, sugar, and salt in a food processor and pulse until combined. Gradually add the butter chunks and pulse until the largest chunks are pea-size. Add the water, 1 tablespoon at a time, and pulse just until the dough begins to clump together against the walls of the processor. Dump the dough out onto a work surface and press together to make a cohesive ball, kneading once or twice if it is falling apart. Divide the dough in half and wrap each in plastic wrap. Refrigerate for 1 hour before using. If you only need enough dough for a single crust, wrap the extra ball in two layers of plastic wrap, put in a resealable plastic bag, and freeze for another time.

Per serving (when serving 6): *562 calories, 9 g protein, 89 g carbohydrates, 20 g total fat, 12 g saturated fat, 1 g fiber, 416 mg sodium*

Per serving (when serving 8): *421 calories, 7 g protein, 67 g carbohydrates, 15 g total fat, 9 g saturated fat, 1 g fiber, 312 mg sodium*

PECAN PIE

I am a little picky when it comes to pecan pie. I like it more nutty than toothachingly sweet, which is why you will find the ratio of nuts to filling a bit higher than is customary for this classic. As a result, the nuts have a tendency to fall out of place when cutting the pie into slices. If you go for a more clean slicing version, decrease the nuts to 2¼ cups. Use only half of Mom's Flaky Pie Dough; wrap the excess in two layers of plastic wrap, put in a resealable plastic bag, and freeze for another time.

ON A WELL-FLOURED surface and with a well-floured rolling pin, roll the dough into a 9" to 10" round. If the rolling pin and work surface quickly become sticky, refrigerate the dough until firm or, using a large spatula or bench scraper, transfer the dough to the pie plate and press it into shape. Crimp the edges and prick the bottom all over with a fork. Refrigerate the pie shell for 20 minutes.

Meanwhile, preheat the oven to 375°F. Place a sheet of parchment paper or foil in the pie shell and fill with pie weights, raw rice, or dried beans. Bake until the edges are lightly golden, about 15 minutes. Remove the weights and paper, and bake until golden and cooked on the bottom and sides, 15 minutes more. Reduce the oven to 350°F.

Combine the sugar and 2½ tablespoons flour in a medium bowl. Add the pecans and whisk in the eggs, yolk, syrup, butter, vanilla extract, and salt. Pour the filling into the crust. Bake until the crust is golden and the filling is set, about 1 hour. Cool completely on a rack for about 2 hours. Serve with whipped cream, if desired.

Per serving (when serving 6): *778 calories, 9 g protein, 80 g carbohydrates, 50 g total fat, 14 g saturated fat, 5 g fiber, 275 mg sodium*

Per serving (when serving 8): *584 calories, 7 g protein, 60 g carbohydrates, 37 g total fat, 11 g saturated fat, 4 g fiber, 206 mg sodium*

YIELD
Makes 1 (8") pie / Serves 6–8

2½ tablespoons all-purpose flour plus additional for dusting work surface

1 recipe Mom's Flaky Pie Dough (opposite page)

½ cup sugar

2½ cups pecans

2 large eggs plus 1 egg yolk, lightly beaten

1 cup grade B or grade A dark amber maple syrup

3 tablespoons unsalted butter, melted

1 teaspoon vanilla extract

⅛ teaspoon kosher salt

Whipped cream for serving (optional)

PANNA COTTA WITH FRUTTI DI BOSCO

This is one of Wolfie's favorite desserts and I have my friend Jessica Harper to thank for it. As the author of her own wonderfully funny cookbook and Web site, *The Crabby Cook,* she can be trusted when she describes this dessert as "the world's easiest and most delicious." I added the frutti di bosco sauce, which, literally translated, is Italian for "fruits of the forest."

TO MAKE THE PANNA COTTA: Pour 1 cup of the milk in a bowl and sprinkle the gelatin over the top. Stir with a fork and let soak until softened, about 5 minutes. Stir again.

Combine the sugar, salt, vanilla bean and seeds, and the remaining 1 cup milk in a large saucepan. Whisk over medium-high heat until the sugar has dissolved, then let the mixture come to a gentle boil. The minute the mixture comes to a boil, remove it from the heat and set aside to cool for 2 minutes. Add the gelatin mixture and stir until dissolved. Add the cream and stir to combine. Remove the vanilla bean.

Set the mixture aside to cool at room temperature, then refrigerate to allow the mixture to thicken, about 30 minutes. Divide equally among eight 4-ounce ramekins and cover each with a piece of plastic wrap pressed directly against the mixture's surface to prevent a skin from forming. Refrigerate until firm, about 5 hours.

TO MAKE THE SAUCE: Just before serving, combine the berries, sugar, and lemon juice in a blender and puree. Taste and adjust the sugar and lemon juice. Strain the mixture through a fine-mesh sieve, forcing it through by pushing and scraping with a rubber spatula.

Spoon the sauce over the panna cotta and serve.

Per serving: *346 calories, 4 g protein, 30 g carbohydrates, 24 g total fat, 15 g saturated fat, 2 g fiber, 88 mg sodium*

YIELD
Makes 8 servings

PANNA COTTA

2 cups cold whole milk

1 tablespoon unflavored gelatin

²⁄₃ cup sugar

⅛ teaspoon kosher salt

½ vanilla bean, split down the middle, seeds scraped out with a paring knife and reserved

2 cups heavy cream

SAUCE

3 cups mixed raspberries, blackberries, and strawberries

2–3 tablespoons sugar

1 tablespoon freshly squeezed lemon juice

CARROT PECAN BREAD

Cooking spray

1¼ cups all-purpose flour plus
    additional for dusting the
    loaf pan

1 teaspoon ground cinnamon

1 teaspoon nutmeg

1 teaspoon ground ginger

½ teaspoon ground cloves

½ teaspoon baking soda

¼ teaspoon baking powder

¼ teaspoon kosher salt

2 large eggs

1 cup sugar

1 tablespoon grated fresh ginger

1 teaspoon vanilla extract

⅓ cup vegetable oil

¾ pound carrots, finely grated

1 cup chopped pecans

When Wolfie was in high school, it seemed as though I was baking this quick bread several times a week. It came in very handy when he and his friends raided the kitchen, ravenous for after-school snacks. I use whatever nuts I happen to have on hand for this; walnuts, almonds, or hazelnuts all work nicely. A food processor makes fast work of grating the carrots, but the small holes of a box grater will do the job, too.

PREHEAT THE OVEN to 375°F. Coat a 8½" x 4½" x 2½" loaf pan thoroughly with cooking spray, then dust well with flour. Tap out the excess.

Sift together the flour, cinnamon, nutmeg, ground ginger, cloves, baking soda, baking powder, and salt into a medium bowl.

Combine the eggs and sugar in the bowl of a stand mixer fitted with the paddle attachment and beat on high speed until the mixture is pale yellow and fluffy, about 7 minutes. Add the fresh ginger and vanilla extract and beat until thoroughly incorporated. Reduce the mixer speed to low and gradually add the oil in a thin stream.

Add the flour mixture in two batches and mix on the lowest speed until just combined. Fold in the carrots and nuts using a rubber spatula. Pour the batter into the prepared pan. Bake until a skewer inserted in the center comes out clean, about 55 minutes. Let the bread cool in the pan on a rack for 15 minutes. Run an offset spatula around the rim of the pan, then turn the loaf out onto the rack and cool 10 minutes more. Cut into ¾"- to 1"-thick slices and serve.

Per serving (when serving 8): *386 calories, 5 g protein, 47 g carbohydrates, 21 g total fat, 3 g saturated fat, 3 g fiber, 211 mg sodium*

Per serving (when serving 10): *309 calories, 4 g protein, 38 g carbohydrates, 17 g total fat, 2 g saturated fat, 3 g fiber, 169 mg sodium*

HELEN'S RICOTTA COOKIES

The first Christmas I spent with Tom's family was memorable for so many reasons, not least of which is his sweet and funny mama's yummy cookies. She makes these in big batches around the holidays and is known to pack up a tinful for anyone who stops by. This recipe yields enough for you to do that, too. Make sure to give the balls of dough a wide berth on the baking sheet, as they flatten and spread in the oven.

TO MAKE THE COOKIES: Preheat the oven to 350°F. Line 2 baking sheets with parchment paper or nonstick silicone liners.

Combine the flour, baking soda, and salt in a small bowl.

Combine the butter and granulated sugar in the bowl of a stand mixer fitted with the paddle attachment, and beat on high speed until light and fluffy. Add the ricotta, eggs, and vanilla extract and beat until thoroughly incorporated. Reduce the mixer speed to low and add the flour mixture, beating until just combined.

Drop the dough by the teaspoon onto the baking sheets, spacing the cookies 2" apart. Bake, rotating and switching the position of the sheets halfway through the baking, until the cookies spread and become golden around the edges, about 12 minutes. Cool on the baking sheets for 5 minutes, then remove the cookies with an offset spatula to the racks and let cool the rest of the way.

TO MAKE THE ICING: Combine the confectioners' sugar, milk, and butter in a medium bowl and whisk together until smooth. Drizzle the icing onto the cooled cookies using a teaspoon, holding it perpendicular to the cookie and letting the icing drip from the tip of the spoon.

Per cookie: *35 calories, 1 g protein, 4 g carbohydrates, 2 g total fat, 1 g saturated fat, 0 g fiber, 17 mg sodium*

YIELD
Makes about 11 dozen

COOKIES
2 cups all-purpose flour

1/2 teaspoon baking soda

1/2 teaspoon kosher salt

1 cup (2 sticks) unsalted butter, softened

1 cup granulated sugar

1 cup plus 1 tablespoon (8 1/2 ounces) ricotta cheese

2 large eggs

1 teaspoon vanilla extract

ICING
1 cup confectioners' sugar

1/4 cup whole milk

2 tablespoons unsalted butter, melted

PIZZELLES

YIELD

Makes 30

1⅓ cups all-purpose flour

⅔ cup sugar

2 teaspoons baking powder

Grated zest of ½ orange

Pinch kosher salt

½ cup (1 stick) unsalted butter, melted and cooled slightly

½ cup whole milk

2 large eggs

2 teaspoons anise extract

Cooking spray

Every Italian American grade-schooler knows pizzelles. They're the quintessential after-school snack. And though Wolfie no longer lives at home, I still make these but only around the holidays. Pizzelles are lovely with a cup of coffee any time of day. You will need a pizzelle iron to make these; you can find one at any good kitchen store.

PREHEAT A PIZZELLE iron. Meanwhile, whisk together the flour, sugar, baking powder, orange zest, salt, butter, milk, eggs, and anise extract in a medium bowl.

Coat the pizzelle iron with cooking spray, then close to continue heating. When the iron is ready, spoon about 1 tablespoon of the batter into each side of the iron. Slowly close and let cook until golden, 50 seconds to 1 minute. Use a small offset spatula to transfer cookies to a wire rack to cool fully. The pizzelles will keep, tightly covered, up to 1 week.

Per cookie: *75 calories, 1 g protein, 9 g carbohydrates, 4 g total fat, 2 g saturated fat, 0 g fiber, 41 mg sodium*

NEAPOLITAN COOKIES

When I was growing up, Christmas began right after Thanksgiving with the start of the cookie-baking marathon. These beautiful layered cookies, which are more cake than cookie, were—and still are—among my favorites. They need to chill in the refrigerator overnight and will take up some space there, so plan accordingly. Use seedless jam to prevent any surprises when you bite into these almond-flavored treats.

PREHEAT THE OVEN to 350°F. Coat three 13" x 9" x 2" jelly-roll pans with cooking spray. Line each pan with wax paper and coat the paper with cooking spray.

Place the almond paste in the bowl of a stand mixer. Break it up into small pieces with a fork. Fit the mixer with the paddle attachment and add the butter and sugar to the bowl. Beat the mixture on high speed until light and fluffy, about 7 minutes. Reduce the speed to medium, add the egg yolks, and beat until incorporated. Turn the mixer off and stir in the flour with a wooden spoon until well combined. Transfer the mixture to a medium bowl.

Clean the mixer bowl thoroughly and fit the mixer with the whisk attachment. Beat the egg whites on high speed until stiff peaks form. Fold the egg whites into the batter until thoroughly blended.

Transfer 1½ cups of the batter to a medium bowl, then transfer another 1½ cups of batter to a second medium bowl. Add the red food coloring to one of the bowls and stir until the batter is tinted throughout. Add the green food coloring to the second bowl and stir until the batter is tinted throughout. Scrape each of the three batters into one of the prepared pans, using the spatula to spread the batter to the edges. Bake, rotating and switching the positions of the pans halfway through, until the edges are golden, 12 to 14 minutes. Let cool in the pans for about 5 minutes, then invert onto cooling racks and allow to cool completely.

(continued)

YIELD

Makes 7 dozen

Cooking spray

8 ounces almond paste

1 cup (2 sticks) unsalted butter, softened

1 cup sugar

4 large eggs, separated

2 cups all-purpose flour

20 drops red food coloring

12 drops green food coloring

¼ cup seedless raspberry jam

¼ cup apricot preserves

6 ounces dark chocolate chips

To assemble, place the green layer on a large cutting board or a large inverted baking sheet lined with wax paper. Spread the raspberry jam evenly over the top. Place the yellow layer on top and spread with the apricot preserves. If there are large chunks of apricots, remove and chop them up to make them more spreadable. Top with the red layer. Cover with plastic wrap and place a heavy cutting board on top to weight it down. Refrigerate overnight.

Place the chocolate chips in a microwaveable bowl and melt in the microwave on low power about 2 minutes. Spread the chocolate on top of the cooled cake and let dry slightly. Trim the rim of the cake with a serrated knife to make clean edges. Cut the cake crosswise into 12 1"-wide strips, then cut lengthwise into $1\frac{1}{4}$" strips. The cookies will keep, covered, up to 1 week.

Per cookie: *71 calories, 1 g protein, 8 g carbohydrates, 4 g total fat, 2 g saturated fat, 0 g fiber, 4 mg sodium*

CANDY CANE COOKIES

These peppermint-flavored Christmas cookies were among my favorites growing up—partly because they filled the house with the most delicious fragrance, and mainly because I loved helping my mother twist the two color strands of dough together into the iconic holiday shape.

YIELD
Makes about 28

1 cup (2 sticks) unsalted butter, softened

1 cup sugar plus additional for sprinkling the cookies

1 large egg

1 large egg yolk

1 teaspoon vanilla extract

2 teaspoons peppermint extract

3 cups all-purpose flour

⅛ teaspoon salt

30 drops red food coloring

COMBINE THE BUTTER and sugar in the bowl of a stand mixer and beat on high speed until light and fluffy. Add the whole egg and yolk and beat until thoroughly incorporated. Scrape down the sides of the bowl with a rubber spatula, then add the vanilla and peppermint extracts and beat until thoroughly mixed. Reduce the speed to low and add the flour and salt, beating until just combined.

Transfer half of the dough to a large bowl. Add the red food coloring and fold in to thoroughly color the dough. Turn both doughs onto individual pieces of plastic wrap and wrap tightly. Refrigerate until firm, at least 2 hours.

Preheat the oven to 375°F. Have ready 2 ungreased baking sheets. Remove 1 tablespoon from each dough and roll each into a snake 6" long. Twist both pieces together, then curve one side so that it looks like a candy cane. Sprinkle with sugar and place on the baking sheet. Repeat with remaining dough, placing cookies 2" apart on the sheet. Bake, switching and rotating the position of the pans halfway through baking, until the cookies are just slightly golden around the edges, 13 minutes. Cool on the baking sheet for 5 minutes, then transfer to a rack to cool completely. The cookies will keep, tightly covered, up to 1 week.

Per cookie: *140 calories, 2 g protein, 18 g carbohydrates, 7 g total fat, 4.5 g saturated fat, 0 g fiber, 14 mg sodium*

Aunt Syl's Anise Twists

YIELD

Makes 5 dozen

2 cups all-purpose flour

1 tablespoon baking powder

½ cup (1 stick) unsalted butter, softened

½ cup sugar

1 large egg

1 teaspoon anise extract

Every time we visit Tom's family in Ohio, a stop at Aunt Syl's is essential. The last time we were there, she had us for coffee and offered, among other delectable treats, these simple but delicious licorice-flavored cookies. They're a staple in many Italian households, but I tend to make them most around the holidays, when the fragrance of anise seems just right for the season.

WHISK TOGETHER THE flour and baking powder in a medium bowl. In the bowl of a stand mixer fitted with the paddle attachment, beat the butter and sugar on high speed until light and fluffy, about 7 minutes. Reduce the mixer speed to low and add the egg. Beat until fully incorporated. Add the anise extract and mix well. Gradually add the flour mixture and beat until a soft, pliable dough forms. Turn the dough out onto a sheet of plastic wrap, shape into a 12" log, and refrigerate for 30 minutes.

Meanwhile, preheat the oven to 375°F. Line 2 baking sheets with parchment paper or nonstick silicone liners.

Working with teaspoon-size pieces of dough, roll them one at a time between the palms of your hands into a 4" snake. Shape the snake into a circle and twist the ends together a few times. Place on a baking sheet. Repeat with the remaining dough, spacing the cookies 2" apart. Bake, switching and rotating the position of the sheets halfway through baking, until golden, about 13 minutes. Cool on racks. Repeat with the remaining dough. The cookies will keep, covered, up to 1 week.

Per cookie: *34 calories, 1 g protein, 5 g carbohydrates, 2 g total fat, 1 g saturated fat, 0 g fiber, 20 mg sodium*

RUSSIAN TEA CAKES

How can something so easy to make—there are only six ingredients—be so melt-in-your-mouth good? Also known as Mexican wedding cookies, these confectioners' sugar–coated balls aren't cakey at all, but rather more like a shortbread with nuts studded throughout.

PREHEAT THE OVEN to 400°F.

Beat the butter and ½ cup of the confectioners' sugar on high speed until light and fluffy, about 7 minutes, in the bowl of a stand mixer fitted with the paddle attachment. Add the vanilla extract and beat until thoroughly incorporated. Reduce the mixer speed to low, add the flour and beat until just combined. Stir in the nuts until incorporated throughout.

Place the remaining 1¼ cups confectioners' sugar on a dinner plate and set aside.

Roll the dough into 1" balls and place 1" apart on 2 ungreased baking sheets. Bake, switching and rotating sheets halfway through baking, until the balls are just toasted around the edges, about 10 minutes. Transfer the cookies to a cooling rack, then immediately roll in the confectioners' sugar to coat entirely. Return the coated cookies to the rack and let cool completely.

Once the cookies have thoroughly cooled, roll them in the confectioners' sugar one more time. The cookies will keep, covered, up to 1 week.

Per cookie: *66 calories, 1 g protein, 7 g carbohydrates, 4 g total fat, 2 g saturated fat, 0 g fiber, 10 mg sodium*

YIELD

Makes about 5 dozen

1 cup (2 sticks) unsalted butter, softened

1¾ cups confectioners' sugar

1 teaspoon vanilla extract

2 cups plus 1 tablespoon all-purpose flour

¼ teaspoon kosher salt

¾ cup finely chopped walnuts

HELEN'S BLACK PEPPER WALNUT BISCOTTI

YIELD

Makes about 30

2¾ cups all-purpose flour

½ teaspoon baking soda

½ teaspoon baking powder

2 teaspoons freshly ground black pepper

Pinch kosher salt

½ cup (1 stick) unsalted butter, softened

1 cup sugar

3 large eggs, at room temperature

2 teaspoons grated orange zest

1½ teaspoons vanilla extract

¼ teaspoon almond extract

1½ cups chopped walnuts, lightly toasted (page 100)

On any given visit, Tom's mom has containers piled up in the pantry, each one filled with a different sweet treat. These twice-baked cookies are a staple in the Vitale household and are served up in the morning with coffee, for late afternoon tea, and after dinner with a sip of grappa. They are eminently dunkable, which makes them a favorite of mine! The orange, vanilla, and almond flavors are intentionally subtle; if you prefer a more intensely flavored cookie, double these ingredients.

SIFT TOGETHER THE flour, baking soda, and baking powder in a medium bowl. Stir in the pepper and salt. Set aside.

In the bowl of a stand mixer fitted with the paddle attachment, beat the butter on high speed until pale and light. Add the sugar and beat until light and fluffy, about 7 minutes. Reduce the speed to low and add the eggs one at a time, beating well after each addition. Add the orange zest and vanilla and almond extracts.

Fold in the flour mixture, then fold in the walnuts. Cover the dough with plastic wrap and refrigerate for 30 minutes.

Preheat the oven to 350°F. Line 2 baking sheets with parchment paper or nonstick silicone liners. Divide the dough in half, place one on each sheet, and shape into two 12" logs, about 2" across. Bake the logs until baked through and lightly browned, 35 minutes. (Leave the oven on.) Let the logs cool for about 10 minutes on the pans, then transfer them carefully to racks to cool 10 minutes more. Using a serrated knife, slice each log on the diagonal into ¾"-thick slices. Arrange the slices, cut side down, on the baking sheets and return to the oven until well toasted, 15 to 20 minutes more. Transfer the biscotti to cooling racks to cool completely. They will keep, tightly covered, up to 1 week.

Per cookie: *142 calories, 3 g protein, 17 g carbohydrates, 8 g total fat, 2.5 g saturated fat, 1 g fiber, 45 mg sodium*

ITALY

I'M PART ITALIAN. TOM is full-blooded Italian. We love Italian food. So when both of us finally cobbled together the same 2 weeks off for vacation, we knew where we wanted to go. It was March 2010, and neither of us had ever been to Italy. Tom had never traveled outside of the United States. Excited, we planned our itinerary, read up on the art and the history, and asked everyone we knew who had already been there where we should eat.

We arrived in Rome ready to do everything—and I think we did. We took in the Colosseum, the Forum, and Palatine Hill. We hit the Pantheon, Trevi Fountain, and the Vatican. We tackled our list of restaurants with equal verve. The history and art was overwhelming, surpassed only by the pasta.

We had the same experience in Florence, where we stared up in awe at Il Duomo, climbed the stairs of the Campanile, walked the Ponte Vecchio, visited the Uffizi, and continued our tour of food stops. By this time, I had started venturing into tiny markets and cheese shops to breathe in the thick aroma of Sottocenere, brunet, mozzarella, provolone, and Gorgonzola. At one place, I bit into a chunk of fresh Parmigiano-Reggiano and moaned, "Can life get better?"

Dinner that night came close. We had made an 8 p.m. reservation at a special place about a 10-minute walk from our hotel. When we set out, I had my trusty map in hand. Forty-five minutes later, Tom and I both were using the GPS on our phones. "It's around the corner," I said. "Which corner?" he asked. Finally, after another 30 minutes in circles, Tom announced, "It's right over there someplace." "Good one," I said. It turned out we were basically standing in front of the restaurant.

We had missed the tiny sign on the door. It was down a flight of stairs leading to a beautiful cellar. But they welcomed us in and fed us for hours. We literally ate like that across Italy, welcomed warmly, fed amazingly, and I didn't gain an ounce. Why? We walked all day, and we didn't snack—a great lifestyle tip.

The following night, life did get better. Tom and I were in our hotel room watching the sunset over the Arno when he proposed. He had planned this for months, but I'm convinced the loving way I had spoken about the pasta chef at the restaurant we'd been at earlier might have made him nervous. We celebrated in the next city on our itinerary, Venice, where we ducked into a little restaurant one afternoon after spotting a plate of cannoli in the window. They were so delicious we went back again that night for dinner. "We don't care what you bring," we said. "Just feed us."

There, in the midst of yet another memorable meal, I asked the restaurant's owner what made everything taste incredible. What did they do special? I wanted to try to duplicate it at home. He smiled. "You liked?" he asked. "I looooooooved," I said. "That is the special ingredient," he said. "Not so secret. You just need to add love—love like the Italians." I glanced at my soon-to-be husband. "We will have fun trying that out at home."

INDEX

Underscored page references indicate boxed text. **Boldfaced** page references indicate photographs.